A SCAR
WHERE GOODBYES
ARE WRITTEN

AN
ANTHOLOGY OF
VENEZUELAN POETS
IN CHILE

a scar
where goodbyes
are written

TRANSLATED AND EDITED BY DAVID M. BRUNSON

~

LOUISIANA STATE UNIVERSITY PRESS
BATON ROUGE

Published by Louisiana State University Press
lsupress.org

Spanish-language edition published as *Una cicatriz donde se escriben despedidas: Antología
de poesía venezolana en Chile,* copyright © 2021 by Libros del Amanecer Ltd., Chile.

LSU Press Paperback Original

Designer: Barbara Neely Bourgoyne
Typefaces: Arno Pro Small Text (text); Frieght Sans Pro (display)

Cover painting: *Ocaso,* by Sara Emanuel Viloria.

Cataloging-in-Publication Data are available from the Library of Congress.

ISBN 978-0-8071-7919-2 (pbk.: alk. paper)
ISBN 978-0-8071-7976-5 (pdf)
ISBN 978-0-8071-7975-8 (epub)

*for the Venezuelan people*
*and all the diasporas*
*of the world*

# CONTENTS

# ACKNOWLEDGMENTS

Compiling and translating this book was a life-changing experience, one that unfolded through five cities, four years, three countries, two major protest movements, and a pandemic. I owe a great many thanks to a great many people. Thank you to the Sturgis Foundation, whose generous grant made my research in Chile possible. Much gratitude to my professors at the University of Arkansas, especially to Geoffrey Brock, for his invaluable input, and to John Duval, for both his brilliance as a translator and for his willingness to bend institutional rules to make sure this project happened. Thank you to Maxi for introducing me to the community of Venezuelan poets in Chile. Thank you to Gladys for putting me in contact with many of these writers and for making Chile my literary home. Thank you to Ivana for her unconditional support, even when I had to evacuate Chile at the start of the pandemic and halt my field research months early, when finishing this anthology seemed impossible. A thank you to my parents for their love and for providing me with their living room during the darkest days of the pandemic, where much of this book was completed.

Thank you to all of my friends in all of my communities in Virginia, Arkansas, Cahuita, and Santiago, who have watched this project evolve from an idea into a book. Thanks as well to Casa Violeta, Smoke and Barrel Tavern, and Playa Negra, places where I spent countless hours hunched over a computer, reading and translating. Many thanks to Libros del Amanecer and Louisiana State University Press for believing in the intellectual, artistic, and human value of the poets featured here and for publishing this book. Finally, I owe an enormous debt of gratitude to these poets, whom I met through all manner of unexpected encounters—at poetry readings, in coffee shops, on social media, on street corners, in classes, and at parties—for their resilience, for their courage, and for trusting me with their remarkable work.

PUBLICATION CREDITS

*ANMLY:* "[The word *city*]" and "[I already recognize myself]," by Miguel Ortiz Rodríguez.

*Asymptote:* "Kakeche," "Intermittence," "[Dead moths]," and "[To burn]," by Eva Tizzani. "River," "City," "Chronicles," and "No Street Will Survive You," by Elizaria Flores.

*Blackbird:* "A Poem Called Country," "Foreigner," and "Hidden Damage," by Georgina Ramírez.

*Copper Nickel:* sections of "Introduction: The Exile of Statistics."

*The Literary Review:* "Patria o muerte—¡Venceremos!" and "Eat Shit, Horseface," by Sara Emanuel Viloria.

*Los Poetas del 5:* "The Scream: A Confusion of Voices," by Gladys Mendía.

*MAYDAY:* "[what impossibility]," "[for my body]," and "everything erased," by Gerardo Arístides Rivodó.

*Nashville Review:* "House," by Sara Emanuel Viloria.

*Temporary Archives: Poems by Women of Latin America,* an anthology published by Arc Publications and Edge Hill University Press: "Billy," "Missvenezuela," "Let the Word Be Spoken," "Cortex," "Father," and "Motel Malamuerte," by Maximiliano Sojo.

*Washington Square Review:* "Memories," by Ivana Aponte.

*Waxwing:* "Migration," "Moles," "Laughter as River," and "Dispatch," by Ivana Aponte.

A SCAR
WHERE GOODBYES
ARE WRITTEN

# INTRODUCTION
## The Exile of Statistics

I first visited Chile as a tourist in July 2018. A colleague of mine in the MFA Program at the University of Arkansas had spent a few years teaching in Santiago, and hearing of my trip, she put me in contact with Maximiliano Sojo, her friend and former coworker—an English teacher and poet from Venezuela. We met for coffee and ended up spending hours discussing poetry's relationship to the political realities of Chile and Venezuela. The differences between these countries are obvious, but the more we spoke, the more I realized how the shadows of dictatorships haunt the lived realities of both.

In his poem "Blackout," Sojo uses the image of an '82 Chevrolet that has been abandoned and riddled with bullet holes, its doors rusted shut on a cliff overlooking a valley abandoned by the people who once lived there. It soon becomes clear that this scene is an extended metaphor for Venezuela's present. Sojo writes that "the machine coughs but doesn't start / all that remains are the parts spared by thieves." Even the last few drops of congealed oil in the engine are "searching for a better life / at the bottom of the cliff." It seemed obvious to me why so many Venezuelans had chosen Chile as a new home—social stability, a strong economy. But Sojo also told me of a side of Chile I had yet to see, a Chile of structural inequality, of poverty tucked out of sight of the city's shimmering towers, of the Mapuche conflict, of wages too low to afford a basic standard of living, of rising tensions between the profoundly stratified social classes. Before we left the coffee shop, Sojo invited me to watch him read that weekend at La Sebastiana, Pablo Neruda's home in Valparaiso. I'd planned to travel to the south of Chile, but as a poet and literary translator, the chance to hear the words of Venezuelan poets in a Nobel laureate's house was too good of an opportunity to pass up. I immediately changed my plans and bought a bus ticket to Valpo.

On the night of the reading, Sojo introduced me to Gladys Mendía, Sara Emanuel Viloria, and Fernando Vanegas. Afterward, we went out to a bar, then spent the evening dancing to Donna Summer in a nightclub. Two weeks later, after meeting numerous other Venezuelans during my travels, Sojo and I met up to talk, realizing that there were enough exiled Venezuelan poets in Chile to curate an anthology of their work. I flew home with a bag full of books, began applying for grants, and won a fellowship from the Sturgis Foundation to undertake this project. A year later, I was on a plane back to Santiago to begin work in earnest.

—

In the United States, a great deal has been said about Venezuela, much of it inaccurate. Some on the left are quick to blame the country's current economic desperation both on US-imposed sanctions and what they perceive as an attempted military coup yet are too slow to condemn the brutally repressive tactics of Nicolás Maduro's illegitimate regime, which have included acts of torture, the imprisonment of political dissidents, and extrajudicial killings (all of which they would harshly criticize under a right-wing dictatorship). The majority of the political right of the United States levy Venezuela's example as a straw man argument against any sort of national legislation that would promote social equality, public health care, progressive taxes, civil rights laws, voting reform, antitrust laws, or union activity, claiming that any of these progressive measures—though routinely enjoyed by social democracies worldwide such as Canada, Denmark, Finland, Germany, New Zealand, Norway, Sweden, and Uruguay—would invariably damn the United States to breadlines. They fail to acknowledge the irrevocable damage caused by the United States' military interventions in practically every country in Latin America as well as their correlation with widespread political instability, leading to the development of authoritarian governments in the region. In this way, our modern right-wing/left-wing rhetoric does too little to distinguish between the authoritarian and democratic social structures that exist independently of our Enlightenment-era terminology. These poems explore the breakdowns of these categorical systems that we've traditionally used in our political discourses and how they relate to the lived experiences of each poet.

Elizaria Flores, in a poem describing Caracas, her former home, begins with the line "The river of my childhood drags along stones and refrigerators, broken tables, useless umbrellas, and anonymous corpses," addressing those lost to violence. She continues by demonstrating several of the contradictions inherent to Caraquenian society: "The city either fasts or fattens, it creates disguises, it roars and curses and it resigns itself. Naked, it embarks on a killing spree or commits suicide. It's a traitor, a backstabber." In 2018, according to the United Nations Human Rights report, the Venezuelan government "registered 5,287 killings, purportedly for 'resistance to authority'. . . . Between 1 January and 19 May [that] year, another 1,569 people were killed, according to Government figures. Other sources suggest the figures may be much higher." Human Rights Watch reports that more than 18,000 people have been killed by security forces between 2016 and 2019. More than 7 million have fled the country in recent years. Due to the repression of information, the exact numbers of refugees, COVID-19 cases, and state-sponsored killings can be difficult to determine. These numbers so often lack names— this is the dehumanizing nature of statisticized violence that the poetry of Venezuelan exiles in Chile resists.

Rising above this violence is not an easy task. To escape it is to be an exile, and exile takes many forms. In the poetry of Gerardo Arístides Rivodó, exile takes on an existential form through the poet's use of Celanesque images. They write:

for my body
exile
a score of snow
want
goodbyes
a lonely storm
the darkness
the dark

In this poem, exile is a blankness, an absence, an unfilled longing, and of course, the dark. For others, exile takes on an explicitly political dimension. For many Venezuelans, Chile has offered a respite from Venezuela's scarcity and hunger but is plagued by its own failing systems, its history of colonization and fascism, and its stratified present that these legacies have created. In 2019, we watched as these frustrations exploded into the *estallido social*, as Chileans bravely fought for a more just country. This fight, however, can be destabilizing in the short term. For some Venezuelans, it was a reminder of the instability and police violence of their home. In her poem "Remnants," Ivana Aponte depicts "Deep wounds in the concrete / There, but ignored." She continues:

Moments of chaos and violence
revive ghosts
of shot-out
skulls
chests
faces

Hatred
with murderous deliberation
sows fear of wandering
a new wandering

Here the old and new ghosts live side by side—the ghosts of the lost, the assassinated, the beaten, the tortured, and the raped. These are the ghosts of state terrorism—a legacy shared by Venezuela, Chile, and the United States. For some, to be an exile is to live in perpetual fear of being displaced again. As the pandemic grinds onward and destabilizes the world, this fear is made real. Many immigrants have fallen through the mesh of the social safety net. The jobs they've lost were not contract based or salaried. Many were part of the underground economy, so they've received no state financial support. Those who can't afford housing—many of them migrants—are living on the streets. Sebastián Piñera's government charged hefty fees to renew travel documents for those left trapped in Chile when the borders closed. New laws have been passed to make the visa application process ever more difficult. Many of these migrants are undocumented. The poems of this anthology stand as a testament to this uniquely difficult era of global crises.

To understand these fears, it is important to understand the changes in the political discourse surrounding the migration process during the past few years, as emigration has surged to exodus. The first people to leave their homeland often belonged to Venezuela's younger, educated generation. This was the generation that came of age during the government of Hugo Chávez and witnessed the slow collapse of their country. This wave began in 2015 as migrants sought new opportunities in professional careers, sent money home to their families, and built lives in more stable countries. Since then, Venezuela's migratory crisis has accelerated, and immigrants have often been met with hostility. Xenophobic rhetoric by leaders such as Donald Trump and Sebastián Piñera as well as presidential candidates such as José Antonio Kast (who, echoing Trump, has called on Chile to "build a ditch" along Chile's northern border to stop the flow of immigrants) has led to new laws that deny temporary protections and visas to refugees while simultaneously using Venezuela's suffering as an example to discredit popular progressive movements within their own countries. Meanwhile, authoritarian left-wing governments in the region, such as those in Cuba and Nicaragua, deny the human rights violations and election fraud under Maduro's regime and view Venezuelan migrants as spies, threats, or traitors. Peru's president, Pedro Castillo, has even hinted at mass deportations of Venezuelan migrants to "return them to the fatherland." Trapped between these different incarnations of xenophobia and extremism, many Venezuelans are left without a country. Whereas the first migrants arrived to jobs, visas, and new lives, today's migrants sleep in metros, parks, and airports and are often the victims of violence. In September 2021 in Iquique, a city in northern Chile, the police forcefully removed an immigrant encampment of dozens of undocumented families from a public park. The next day, Chilean nationalists attacked the families and burned their belongings while singing the national anthem.

Given this reality, what is the role of the poet? While collecting these poems, I began to think of the differences between the reportage of journalism and the reportage of poetry. While the importance of good journalism is undeniable, it at times fails to truly encapsulate the hearts and minds of its subjects—especially when an unfathomably large number of humans are involved. The reportage of journalism instead relies on metanarrative as its primary mode of discourse, but this comes with its own set of shortcomings. The phrase "seven million Venezuelan migrants are now living abroad" fails to encapsulate the personal, intellectual, and emotional histories that hide behind the thin veneer of statistics. It fails to account for the emotional weight of watching a country slowly fail, of watching friends and family disappear one by one, of leaving a country behind forever. The phrase "5,287 extrajudicial killings" can't account for the story of each life lost or the emotional toll on the lives left behind, of daily commutes that pass by jails and interrogation sites, of the ever-present hunger. The poems of this anthology present a different kind of reportage, that of the migrant, one who struggles to find balance between being both a witness bearer and a victim of atrocity, and of rising above this trauma as a fully realized human, one who has lived these experiences but who will not be defined by victimhood. The migrant poet struggles with being a participant in a mass exodus and with retaining their own individuality, of rising up to be more than just a number. In one poem, titled "Patria o muerte—¡Venceremos!" Sara Viloria writes:

> Here we are, a family name lost to statistics
> another foreign name
> but back there
> > back there
> we are the news, the front page of the paper

Beyond even politics, these are poems of reclamation, poems that fight to address the timeless realities of the heart—joy, sorrow, love, heartbreak, anger, hope—the wind that blows through each of us, our voices, our irrevocable humanity. In a poem aptly titled "The Scream," Gladys Mendía writes:

> oh my daughters why don't I believe?
> why do my arms always drop?
> where's my voice?

I often feel the same way during these moments of crushing injustice. If, in these times, the reading and writing of poetry is an act of resistance, then reading poetry from other voices—across racial, socioeconomic, cultural, and national lines—becomes an act of rebellion. Though the lived experiences of these poets may be different, I believe the truth that these poems breathe is universal. By reading and collecting these poems and by speaking with the poets (many of whom I now have the privilege of calling friends), I have gained guidance and insight that I would not have been able to find within my own culture or my own literary tradition. I hope that you as readers have a similar experience. It seems things will get worse before they get better, but like the poets featured here, we still need to cling to that which keeps us human. We need to empathetically reimagine the world, and we need to listen. Through this, we might survive. We might even flourish. As Mendía writes in "The Scream":

there are as many rooms as heartbeats
there are as many windows as mirrors
the wind becomes infuriated with the curtains
with the picture frames
with the shape of the wardrobe
and they fall
they fall because everything falls eventually

there is a brightness inside
sisters
there is a pure brilliance unlike anything else

SARA EMANUEL VILORIA

## Venceremos

Me inscribí al partido socialista a los 16 años
viví el florecer de un estado fallido
        antes de perder la virginidad
regamos los votos con nuestras voces
la revolución era nuestra cara de frente
al *sticker* del Che que el abuelo puso junto al retrovisor
y eso fue antes del secuestro
¿quiénes éramos nosotros?

La sangre nos corre hasta los codos
sabemos que no somos los malos
pero puede haber daño en una idea
        sí puede haberlo
porque hablar de vajillas de plata y de los pobres, tía
es creer que una no es pobre
y todos los caramelos de licor en el cuenco de cristal
no nos quitaron el sabor de la última Navidad
cuando mucha gente no comía
pero nuestros estómagos no rugían de hambre
entonces
¿quiénes éramos nosotros?

La generación de relevo que se fue del país
la artista promesa que nunca pintó al tío Roberto
el fantasma de la niña que celebró la victoria de Chávez
        febrero del 99
porque aun no sabía que el niño Jesús no existía

¿quiénes éramos nosotros?
cuando nos gritábamos, madre
y no podíamos ponernos de acuerdo
y yo te decía que me apuntaron con un arma
y que tenía miedo

## Patria o muerte—¡Venceremos!

*Rallying cry used by Fidel Castro during the Cuban Revolution*

I joined the socialist party at sixteen
I lived through the flowering of a failed state
  before losing my virginity
we watered the votes with our voices
the revolution was our face in front
of the Che sticker that Grandpa stuck on the rearview mirror
but that was before he was held hostage
who were we?

We're up to our elbows in blood
we know we're not the bad guys
but ideas can be dangerous
   yes, they can be dangerous
because speaking of silver spoons and the poor, Auntie
is to believe that we aren't poor
and all the liquor chocolates in our crystal bowl
couldn't mask the bitter taste of last Christmas
when many people didn't eat
but our stomachs didn't roar with hunger
so then
who were we?

The generation of change that left the country
the aspiring artist who never painted her uncle Roberto
the ghost of the girl that celebrated the victory of Chávez
  February '99
because I didn't even know that El Niño Jesús wasn't real

Who were we?
Mother, when we screamed at each other
when we couldn't agree
and I told you that I was afraid
that I'd had a gun pointed at me

entonces un chofer me llevaba y me traía
pero yo no sé a dónde iba
ni quiénes éramos nosotros

¿Quiénes éramos?
¿dónde vas, tío, todos los días
con un traje de follaje verde sin flores?
¿qué se siente perder el control de una frontera?
¿qué es una frontera?
una cicatriz
donde se escriben despedidas

¿Piensas en nosotros?
dime que piensas en nosotros
porque la imagen del presidente dándote la mano me dio vergüenza
y es una fotografía que no quiero en mi memoria, pero la tengo
como el sueño de mi tía,
recostada en la tumba de Chávez
con su cabello rojo como Dánae
recitando nuestros nombres
aunque no lo sabemos
aún no sabemos
¿quiénes éramos nosotros?

Aquí somos un apellido que se pierde en la estadística
otro nombre ajeno
pero allá
            allá
somos la noticia, la plana del periódico
que subscribe las promesas
el ministerio de la suprema felicidad del pueblo
ese lugar existe y también existe Ernesto
el primo que honra su uniforme
traficando gasolina
se me incendian las encías
cuando mastico su nombre
pero lo quiero, más que a los otros

and I had to be escorted by a bodyguard
but I don't know where I was going
or who we were

Who were we?
where do you go, Uncle, every day
in your suit of green foliage where no flowers grow?
what does it feel like to lose control of a border?
what is a border?
a border is a scar
where goodbyes are written

Do you think of us?
tell me that you think of us
because I'm ashamed of the image of the president shaking your hand
I don't want to remember this photograph, but here it is
just like my dream of my aunt
with her hair as red as Klimt's Danaë
lying down on Chávez's grave
reciting our names
although we don't know
we still don't know
who were we?

Here we are, a family name lost to statistics
another foreign name
but back there
                    back there
we are the news, the front page of the paper
which endorses their promises
The Vice Ministry of Supreme Social Happiness
a place that exists just as Ernesto exists
my cousin who honors his uniform
trafficking gasoline
that sets fire to my gums
every time I chew on his name
but I love him more than the rest

Porque ellos también son familia
aunque siempre estuvieron del lado derecho
paseaban en yates en Miami
nunca tocaron libros
sus hijas jugaban a ser princesas Disney
camisas del Real Madrid
relojes Mulco
¿Y quienes éramos nosotros?

Era mi abuela sirviéndole café
a un Chávez desconocido en campaña
¿o éramos la consigna de la espada de Bolívar
que iba a atravesar América Latina
pero nos atravesó a nosotros?

    *Sabana, mañana cuando me vaya,*
        *Te quedarás tan solita . . .*

¿Y quienes éramos?
porque hoy somos el partido
estamos partidos
hemos partido
       estamos seccionados
  divididos
y cada vez que me hablan de política
quiero llorar
porque la verdad es que sí duele
y una evita pensar en palabras lastimeras
       como silencio
pero el hermano de mi primer amor
está preso por traición a la patria
¿y cómo puede traicionarse algo
que ya no reconocemos?
¿cuántas madres besan los barrotes de la duda
porque sus hijos protestaron?

But they are also family
though they will always be right-wing
sailing yachts through Miami
never opening books
their daughters dressed as Disney princesses
wearing Real Madrid jerseys
Mulco watches
and who were we?

My grandmother serving coffee to an unknown Chávez
on his first campaign?
or the mandate of Bolívar's sword
which cut across Latin America?
but did it also cut through us?

    *Savannah, tomorrow when I go,*
       *You will be left so alone* [1]

And who were we?
because today we're The Party
we're partitioned
we've parted
      we're halved
    divided . . .
and every time we talk politics
I want to cry
because the truth is that yes it hurts
and one avoids thinking in mournful words
      like *silence*
but the brother of my first love
is locked away for treason to la Patria
how can one betray something
that they no longer recognize?
no longer loving the sacrifice of their children
how many mothers kiss the prison bars?

---

1. Lyric from "Sabana" by Simón Díaz, an iconic Venezuelan folk singer.

y se arrancan
                y se comen los cabellos
                                cabello
aunque ese nombre ya ni se tranza
ni se trenza
        que estamos disueltos
                desarraigados
abiertos
por todo el mundo
hablando inglés, árabe, holandés
aprendiendo nuevos verbos
sin nombrar lo que hemos hecho
¿quiénes éramos nosotros?

Los nietos de los terratenientes
que construyeron el país
                        con las manos negras de petróleo
porque nuestras huellas
qué importa cuantas veces
                        marquemos nuestras huellas
en las líneas de racionamiento
        o en aduanas y aeropuertos
igual tenemos agujas en las huellas de los dedos
                        y dejamos charcas de sangre
cada vez abrazamos
                        en las esquinas
        y los espejos donde nos convencemos
que no somos extraños
        que no somos como ellos
                        nos vamos tiñendo de rojo
y aunque aún no nos toca
        la Revolución del Terciopelo
todavía no llegamos a saber

they rip out their god-given hair
     and eat it in rebellion
          though Diosdado Cabello's name
cannot be berated
or unbraided
   and we are dissolved
       uprooted
dispersed
across the entire world
speaking English, Arabic, Dutch
learning new verbs
but still not naming what it is we've done
who were we?

The grandchildren of the landowners
who built the country
               with oil-blackened hands
and our footprints . . .
what does it matter how many times
          we mark our tracks
in the ration lines at the supermarket
   or in customs and airports?
it's needles pressed into the palms of our hands
          and we leave pools of blood
each time we hug
          on the street corners
   and in the mirrors where we convince ourselves
that we're not so strange
   that we're not like them
               but we leave, stained red
and the Velvet Revolution
   still has not reached us
and still we don't know—

## Casa

Cáscaras de cebolla morada en la cocina
un ramo de peonias
reciclo incendios
mis colillas de hierba
en las cenizas vencejos que no quieren ser fénix
en la tina las huellas de las madrugadas sola
agua en las copas
      vino en las tazas
         café amargo en mi lengua

un condimento: curiosidad

La casa es mi laboratorio
las hormigas huyen
      soy una tirana
pero la luz permanece
los prismas me acarician las pestañas
las orejas, los muslos
las tablas crujen
pero nunca tuve
tanta certeza sobre mis pasos

Los gatos pasean
         me lamen

Estamos en guerra con los autobuses
los ignoramos
aceptamos el ruido
en casa siempre aceptamos

Bajamos el ritmo, nos consumimos
mis almohadas sueñan a lo bonzo
mis sueños se extinguen
¿cuáles son?

## House

Red onion skins in the kitchen
a bouquet of peonies
I recycle fire
from the stubs of smoked joints
in the ashes, swifts who never wished to be a phoenix
in the bathtub, traces of early mornings alone
water in cups
        wine in glasses
            bitter coffee on my tongue

curiosity: a seasoning

The house is my laboratory
the ants flee
        I am a tyrant
but the light lingers
prisms caress my eyelashes
my ears and my thighs
the boards creak
but I've never felt so sure
of my steps

The cats prowl around
                they lick me

We are at war with the buses
we ignore them
we accept the noise
at home we always accept

We slow down, we consume ourselves
my pillows dream of self-immolation
my dreams are extinguished
what are they?

Alguien trajo de Brasil cigarrillos raros
libros de páginas hermosas, las hojas
del cilantro acarician la ventana
las lentejas se cuecen junto a la tetera
al atardecer
la monotonía es una isla
el mundo se detiene

Giro y doy traspiés sobre mi sombra
para alguien que solo conoce los naufragios
es irrelevante cuantos ríos hay cerca de casa

La fuente de agua de los gatos
suena apacible
me lavo
como Sexton
*como acuarela, soy lavable*
y acaso el reflejo del piso que se limpia
acusa que existo

Someone brought me rare cigarettes from Brazil
books with beautiful pages, cilantro leaves
caress the window
the lentils cook next to the teapot
at sunset
monotony is an island
where the world stops

I turn and stumble over my shadow
for someone who only knows shipwrecks
it doesn't matter how many rivers are close to home

The cat's water fountain
sounds gentle
I wash myself
like Sexton
*I am a watercolor, I wash off*
and perhaps the reflection on the polished floor
accuses me of existing

## DesMadre

*a mi madre*

Me rompí las rodillas probando el whisky de mis tíos
llamé a la tv, la cuenta del teléfono fue mi culpa
rompí tu pañuelo de seda corriendo entre cujíes
el tatuaje fue a los 15, no a los 17
consumí LSD en casa
mientras estabas en Colombia
casi chocamos en el auto cuando nos escapamos a Mérida
no voté por Chávez aunque puse en riesgo tu trabajo
mis amigos se drogaban en la terraza
el condón roto era de Pedro
me metí con tu amigo
preferí encerrarme que verte
porque te culpo de muchas cosas
inventé tu peor versión
para castigarte por lo que yo no sabía decirme
has soportado con tanto amor en silencio
porque no sabías nada de esto
y yo solo sé decir que te amo profundamente
que atesoro todas estas cicatrices
y el jersey celeste que me tejiste
a pesar del desmadre

## Shitshow

*for my mother*

I broke my knees after trying my uncles' whiskey
I called the number on TV, the telephone bill was my fault
I tore your silk handkerchief running between the cují trees
my first tattoo was at fifteen, not seventeen
I ate LSD in the house
while you were in Colombia
we almost crashed the car when we ran off to Mérida
I didn't vote for Chávez, which put your job at risk
my friends got high on the terrace
the broken condom was Pedro's
I fooled around with your friend
I hid in my room because I didn't want to see you
because I blame you for many things
I invented the worst version of you
punishing you for what I didn't know how to tell myself
you have endured, with all of your love, in silence
because you knew nothing of this
all I know how to say is that I love you deeply
that I wear all of these scars
beneath the sky-blue sweater that you knitted me
in spite of this shitshow

## Amy

*For you I was the flame*
*Love is a losing game*

Tuve este sueño
en el que era una cerilla
con dos cabezas
y ardía
como las estrellitas
que papá ponía en mis manos
cuando el mundo no era oscuro
      la infancia olía a pólvora
y los susurros del mundo
se escuchaban en una barrita de alambre
destinada a irradiar y morir

Siempre autodestructiva
nunca dejé de ser aquella niña
que asomaba la cabeza
en las fogatas
porque quería besar al fuego
aunque los huesos de las reses
se calcinaran entre las ramas
donde las chispas buscan su origen
por ti soy la llama

## Amy

*For you I was the flame*
*Love is a losing game*

I had this dream
where there was a match
with two heads
and it burned
like the crackling stars
that Dad pressed into my hands
when the world was not dark
      childhood smelled of gunpowder
and all the sighs of the world
could be heard in sparklers
destined to radiate and die

Always self-destructive
I never stopped being that girl
who poked her head
into the blaze
because she wanted to kiss fire
even though the beef bones
burned among the branches
where sparks search for their origin
for you I am the flame

# Nínive

Jonás
¿qué se siente ser escupido del techo de la ballena?
masticar con las encías rotas
todo un continente
sin saber digerirlo
nadar, romperte los nudillos
subir un helicóptero, cruzar un país
como lo hacían en el holocausto
niños destrozados por caramelos de ciruela

¿Qué es el océano, Jonás?
¿Qué países se inventan las mareas cuando suben?
¿Qué discurso se aloja sobre el niño refugiado
que naufraga y se queda dormido para siempre en la arena
con la oreja sobre una caracola
que reproduce el silencio del mundo?

¿A quién le pides deseos,
si te quitaron de un tajo 7 u 8 estrellas del pecho?
¿Cuándo vas a preguntar por los amigos que no conociste
y comparten los mapas de tus rodillas?
¿Cuántas veces al día caminas de derecha a izquierda,
sin entenderte, Jonás?

¿Cuándo llamas a la memoria para fundar un juego?
¿Por quién tomas partido
cuando la ventana de tu nueva casa
da hacia una pared vestida de sombras
y la luz como la conocías
se extingue?

## Nineveh

Jonah, how did it feel
when you were spat from the roof of the whale?
chewing with broken gums,
everything a continent
you don't know how to digest
swimming, breaking your knuckles
climbing into a helicopter, crossing a country
like they did in the Holocaust,
children crushed for plum candies?

What is an ocean, Jonah?
What countries create the rising tides?
What speech floats above the refugee child
whose raft sank, who sleeps forever in the sand
resting his ear on a seashell
where the world's silence rings?

Who do you wish upon?
Shall they gouge 7 or 8 stars from your chest?
When will you ask about the friends you never knew
and share with them the maps of your knees?
How many times per day do you walk between the right and the left
without understanding yourself, Jonah?

When do you draw upon memory for a game?
Who do you side with
when the window of your new house
faces a wall draped in shadows
and the light as you once knew it
is extinguished?

¿Qué es el mar, Jonás
sino esa herida que se desplaza por tus mejillas?
cuando enciendes el noticiario
y ves un ejército
que se quedó con tus Legos
pero no saben construir naciones

What is the sea, Jonah
if not this wound that drips down your cheeks?
When you burn the newsreel
and see an army
that steals your Legos
but doesn't know how to build nations

# Tromba

¿Recuerdas? aquella vez en el pueblo de la playa cuando pasó una viejita y te dijo:

—Hija usted sí es bonita.

Y a mí me dijo:

—Y usted sí tiene suerte.

—LUIS MANUEL PIMENTEL

El mar era la casa,
éramos ola
rodeábamos a los surfistas con nuestras risas adolescentes
naufragamos en litorales ahora perdidos
nos gustaba decir que las ventanas
eran de viento,
y el viento se escupía de nuestras bocas
húmedas de cocuy, ávidas de sed

Las paredes terrosas tendían nuestras sombras al sol
el salitre se escurría en nuestros poros
deshidratados, dos niños esculpidos con silicatos
salíamos a mirar el horizonte
apostados entre los cactus
—no solo los peces tienen espinas—
también los erizos que pisamos
en el cabo
(y las palabras)

## Waterspout

Do you remember that time in the beach town when an old woman
passed us and she said to you: "Child, you are beautiful"?
And then she turned to me and said,
"You sir, have good luck."
—LUIS MANUEL PIMENTEL

The sea was our house
we were a wave
we bathed in the surf with teenage smiles
we were shipwrecked along now-lost coastlines
we liked to say that the windows
were made of wind
and that we spat the wind from our mouths
wetlands of cocuy, dying of thirst

The earthen walls stretched our shadows to the sun
the salt crusted into our pores
dehydrated, we were two children sculpted of silicate
we gazed at the horizon
that stretched between the cactuses
—fish aren't the only spined things—
also the sea urchins we stepped on
at the cape
(and our words)

# Missing

En esta historia, te escapas
en esta historia, sangras
en esta historia, sobrevives.
—CAITLYN SIEHL

Cuando veía los rostros desaparecidos
en los cartones de leche
no imaginaba que tampoco estaría
ajena
pérdida

Vista desde mi pasaporte
jamás pensé que sería
una de esas mujeres
impresas en cartón
tal vez mutiladas
ajenas, sonrientes

Dando rienda a la memoria
desde aquella despensa llena
de productos canadienses
al borde del cereal
un domingo en la mañana
desapareciendo en una mesa sin país
frente a un cartón arrugado
al que le sacaron toda la leche
y la música del Miss Venezuela anunciando
desde el televisor un nuevo amanecer

# Missing

In this story, you escape
in this story, you bleed
in this story, you survive.
—CAITLYN SIEHL

When I would see their disappeared faces
on the boxes of milk
I imagined that I'd also be either
    alien
       or loss

Seen from my passport
I never thought I'd matter enough
to be one of those women
printed on cardboard
mutilated perhaps
missing, smiling

giving rein to memory
from some pantry full
of Canadian products
next to the cereal
one Sunday morning
disappearing into a table without a country
in front of the crumpled cardboard box
after they've drunk all the milk
as from the TV, Miss Venezuela's music
announces a new dawn

# Maculada

## I

Mamá me pagaba con helados
debía permanecer con las manos quietas
había que sacar tantos moldes de yeso
como fuese posible
devolverles a las vírgenes del pueblo
sus pequeñas manos caídas por los besos
de las ancianas

## II

A los 13 años me tiré de la ventana
cuerpo ensordecido
el pavimento, caja musical
los talones golpearon el bombo de la tierra
la columna desecha entre crisálidas
mi infancia bautizada en mariposas de sangre
aplaudieron las vírgenes

## III

Celebró la niña que descubrió el dolor del blanco
en las manos de un pintor viejo
aprenda señor a llorar sobre su leche derramada
la adolescente que se tatuó *arder*
y *oscuridad* en el mismo brazo

# Maculate

### I

Mom paid me in ice cream
to keep my hands from scratching
so many plaster casts had to be removed
as if it were possible
to give the village virgins back their hands
that had fallen beneath the weight
of the old ladies' kisses

### II

When I was thirteen I jumped out the window
my body gone deaf
the pavement, a music box
my heels struck the earth's bass drum
my spine cast off in that cocoon
my childhood baptized in butterflies of blood
the virgins applauded

### III

the girl discovered the pain of the white page
in the hands of an old painter and celebrated
learn how to cry over spilt milk sir
the teenager tattooed *burning*
and *darkness* on the same arm

## Gasoline guillotine

*(Cortarse el cabello es un acto de amor a lo bonzo)*

Vieras cuán fácil es incendiarse
cuán sutil puede ser destejerse la cabellera
y cortar fibra a fibra el pasado

Hacer hogueras con trenzas, crujir pestañas como chispas
arder labios como brasas, dedos como pinzas
ojos que llueven como llamas

Tan fácil es extinguirse y aniquilar el mito del fénix
delinear circuitos de pólvora entre la nuca y la sombra
de cabellos vírgenes en la frente
abrir el vacío con un "crj . . . crj . . . crj" constante
apagar con vehemencia las humaredas malva que se asoman al suelo
y no permitir que un solo cabello susurre mientras se desplaza
desde la cueva de una oreja hasta el
hombro *permiso, no quiero morir*

Vieras cuán fácil es hacerse añicos comenzando por la cabeza
quemar cristales, perlas, memorias cayendo de peñascos
coronas de flores, alambrados desérticos
agujas de reloj contándome los años
cabello a cabello, minuto a pasado, demolición tras desencanto.

No imaginas cuántos escombros caben
en 23 centímetros de cabellera
incendiándose en el lavamanos
no tienes idea de cómo desapareció ayer
pompeya de la faz de la tierra a las 23 horas

## Gasoline Guillotine

*(Cutting your hair is an act of self-immolating love)*

You'll see how easy it is to burn yourself down
how gentle it can be to unweave your hair
and cut away the past, fiber after fiber

Setting bonfires with braids, eyelashes crackling like sparks
burning lips like embers, fingers like tongs
eyes that rain like flames

It's so easy to extinguish and annihilate the myth of the phoenix
outlining circuits of gunpowder between the nape of the neck and the shadow
of virgin hair in the front
opening the void with a constant "crackle . . . crackle . . . crackle . . ."
vehemently extinguishing the clouds of mauve smoke that appear from the floor
not allowing a single hair to whisper—while falling
from ear's cave
to the shoulder—*excuse me, I don't want to die*

You'll see how easy it is to destroy, beginning with your head
burning crystals, pearls, memories falling from mountaintops
crowns of flowers, barbed wire fences in the desert
the clock's hands counting my years
hair by hair, minute by minute, demolition after disenchantment

You can't imagine how much rubble fits
in twenty-three centimeters of hair
catching fire in the sink
you'll have no idea how, yesterday at 11:00 p.m.
Pompeii disappeared from the face of the earth

## Yegua tiramierda

Cuando pienso en libertad,
Pienso en Isla, mi yegua,
Y pienso en una fotografía de mi abuela,
Bellísima a sus 17 años,
De esos días ella recuerda,
Que un hombre la llamó yegua tiramierda.

Y pienso en la libertad como la belleza,
Presta a arder, a ser incinerada,
Atacada por todos sus fuertes.

Yegua tiramierda,
Es sinónimo de una mujer paciente,
Presta a dejarse pasar por el tiempo.

Comparto con las mujeres de mi familia,
La fascinación por no querer comprender el tiempo,
Mamá teje, como Penélope,
Con el fin único de esperar,
Mi hermana religiosa mide el tiempo por la experiencia,
Mi abuela tiene una eternidad triste en el pecho.

Isla, la yegua, tiene años que no se deja montar,
Nadie pondrá un reloj en el bonito rombo de su frente,
Andar una, dos, siete horas,
Con el tiempo de la humanidad tatuado en el entrecejo,
Es vivir muriendo.

Domar a la belleza,
Reducir la existencia a pastar pensando en el horizonte,
Sin pensar en sí misma,
Con una silla en la espalda,
El cuerpo de un hombre arqueándola bajo su peso,
Con un brazo torciéndole el cuello,
Y una sombra ajena, haciendo más grande su sombra.

## Eat Shit, Horseface

When I think of freedom
I think of Isla, my mare,
And I think of a photo of my grandmother,
Gorgeous at seventeen.
She remembers, in those days,
When a man told her to *eat shit, horseface.*

And I think of freedom, like beauty,
Ready to burn—incinerated,
Attacked with full force.

*Eat shit, horseface* means
Being a patient woman,
Given to drifting through time.

Like the women of my family
I do not want to understand time.
Mama knits, like Penelope,
Waiting her only purpose.
My religious sister measures time by experience.
My grandmother has an eternity of sadness in her chest.

Isla, my horse, has not allowed anyone to ride her for years,
Nobody will place an hourglass on her forehead's handsome diamond.
Pacing for one, two, seven hours
With humanity's time tattooed between her furrowed brows—
This is to live dying.

Taming beauty,
Her existence reduced to grazing, contemplating the horizon,
Without thinking of herself
With a saddle on her back,
Arching beneath the weight of a man's body,
With an arm twisting her neck,
And a stranger's shadow making her shadow grow.

La libertad, es un golem que transcribe a capricho,
Las palabras que ponen en su boca.

Yegua tiramierda,
Es aceptar ser el blanco de la mierda de otros,
Es mi abuela, es mi madre,
Y soy yo, y mis primas,
Y es Isla, que es de ella,
Que no es mía.

Freedom is a golem that, on a whim,
Transcribes the words placed in its mouth.

*Eat shit, horseface* is
To accept being the target for other people's shit,
To be my grandmother, my mother,
And to be me, and my cousins,
And Isla, who belongs to herself,
Not to me.

## Kakeche

Estoy temblando en el lugar desconocido. El río tiene flores, no arrastra piedras, es una oleada noble cubierta de pieles negras. Estoy en el ruido de esta ciudad, me desbordo. Cerré los ojos y gritaron *gualmapu*. Venía de lejos, lo único que visualicé fue la cordillera bañada de nieve, se me enfriaron los huesos y al mismo tiempo la ciudad me empezó a abrazar. Lloré por verme lejos de casa, se me acercó un hombre y escuché *entrequen*. Me había vuelto ceniza y me fundí en el asfalto de estas calles. A mi oído susurró una mujer—*kakeche* nunca, eres nuestra—.

## Kakeche

*—with words from the Mapudungun*

I'm shuddering in a strange place. The river doesn't have flowers, doesn't drag stones, it's a noble surge covered in black skins. I'm inside this city's noise, I overflow. When I close my eyes, they shout *Gualmapu*.[1] I came from afar. I only imagined a ridgeline bathed in snow, which froze my bones as the city embraced me. So far from home, I cried. A man approached. I heard *entrequen* as I turned to ash and melted into these asphalt streets.[2] Into my ear, a woman whispered, "*Kakeche* never, you are ours."

*Kakeche* means "stranger, foreigner, one from another place."

1. Ancestral land.

2. *Entrequen* means "ash."

## [La lengua me sabe a mar]

La lengua me sabe a mar

a dientes rotos

a mamá

a la casa de Puerto Cabello

lengua costrosa
adormecida

En mi boca
concha de mar polvorienta
me recuerda lo lejos que está la casa

[My tongue tastes of sea]

My tongue tastes of sea

of broken teeth

of mom

of our house at Puerto Cabello


scabbed tongue
numb


In my mouth
dusty seashell
reminding me how far away my home

## [En este espacio]

En este espacio
soy
la cama llena de migajas
los hombros cansados

soy
animal quieto
sobre sábanas blancas

[In this space]


In this space
I am
the bed full of crumbs
tired shoulders

I am
motionless animal
on white sheets

## Intermitencia

La ciudad me cae encima. Me punza el pecho.

María Lionza se parte en dos
y Sorte se queda sin reina.
    Doncella de mirada hundida,
        Danta con el ombligo lleno de gusanos.

Quebranto de ciudades desahuciadas
        ahogo del no-retorno

Parir.
Huir.
Retornar.

Esta ciudad cabra agazapada,
           luz intermitente.
           Garganta llena de piedras.
      Grito.
Jadea.

        País en el nombre del padre,
     con un puñado de cruces en la boca.

## Intermittence

The city falls over me. It punches my chest.

The goddess María Lionza is cleaved,
Mount Sorte left queenless.
     Hollow-eyed maiden,
         a tapir's gut filled with larvae.

Shattered cities, evicted,
         drowning in no-return.

Birth.
Escape.
Return.

This city: a cowering goat,
         intermittent light.
         Throat filled with stones.
     A shout.
Panting.

         Country in the name of the father,
       a fistful of crosses in its mouth.

## [Taras muertas]

Taras muertas,
lobos en el jardín
de hombres enterrados,
polillas rojas sobre mi rostro
hacen el grito.

Me nombran:
tierra seca soy,
tamarindo muerto,
mango podrido en la tierra.
El mundo es un punto pequeñísimo
sobre mi cuerpo,
ruido caído del árbol.
Soy ese sonido vacío.

[Dead moths]


Dead moths,
wolves in the garden
of buried men,
the red wings covering my face
turn into a scream.

They name me:
dry land, I am
dead tamarind,
mango rotting in the soil.
The world is a speck
on my body,
noise falling from the tree.
I am that empty sound.

## [Arder]


Arder
en todos tus bosques

[sin ceniza]

Estar en tu pecho
encendida

Solárium sagrado
Ángel que me habita
luz de pájaro en mis ramas

Arde hasta que ningún polvo
sobre la tierra nos pueda.

## [To burn]

To burn
in all your forests

      [without ash]

on your chest
ignited

Sacred solarium
Angel within me
a bird's light on my branches

Burn with us across the land
until not even dust is left.

## [Grita el cuerpo que soy]

Grita el cuerpo que soy
en el ensueño

duermo sobre guacucos y flores

                                       No me despiertes

Para volver
al cuerpo
roto

[This body that I am screams]

This body that I am screams
in reverie

I sleep on clams and flowers

                              Don't wake me up

To return
to the broken
body

## [Aquí habito]

Aquí habito,
en la ciudad silenciosa que me retrata.

                         En la casa llena de mí
y del mutismo de las flores.

[Here I dwell]


Here I dwell,
in the silent city that takes my portrait.

                        In the house full of me
and the muteness of the flowers.

MIGUEL ORTIZ RODRÍGUEZ

## [Santiago se abre]

Santiago se abre
como una herida
   reciente,
como una flor
   de carne.
Santiago se niega
en su reflejo,
   en su sísmica pisada.
La cordillera anuncia
lo vivo
   con velocidad de vértigo.

## [Santiago opens up]

Santiago opens up
like a fresh
    wound,
like a flower
    of flesh.
Santiago refuses itself
in its own reflection,
    in its seismic footprint.
The cordillera declares
*the living*
    with vertigo's velocity.

## [La palabra *ciudad*]

La palabra *ciudad*
esconde un polvo
inherente a lo animal

Una ciudad es siempre
   biológica

Una ciudad nace   caga    come
     agoniza
   se sabe hueso pulcro
y sepulcro de todos los muertos

La palabra *ciudad*
   adolece de un signo real

La palabra *ciudad*
   es siempre un mapa extinto
un calco de lo que debía ser

La palabra *ciudad* se erige
   como un monumento vertebrado
   nacido de la propia sangre de lo vivo
   una ciudad como una inmensa selva
   una casa
      como un nido
      como un panal
      a punto de ser quemado

## [The word *city*]

The word *city*
hides
an animal dust

A city is always
   biological

A city is born   shits   eats
      agonizes
   knows itself as fleshless bone
and tomb of all of the dead

In the word *city*
   there's no real sign

The word *city*
   is always an extinct map
an outline of what it should be

The word *city* erects itself
   as a vertebral monument
   born of the same blood as the living
   a city like an immense jungle
   a house
      like a nest
      like a honeycomb
      about to be burned

# [Ya me reconozco]

Ya me reconozco
en las calles de Santiago
en lo abrumadoramente contradictorio
          de su sangre,
por supuesto en la insurgencia,
          en sus paredes rayadas,
en la velocidad imperdonable
          de las micros
en sus esquinas ruinosas
          o incendiadas,
en las madrugadas heladas
          y el merkén.
Creo en Santiago
como en mí mismo,
          bestia nacida
de la afrenta. Creo
en sus zorzales, en
los graznidos del tiuque
          resonantes de verano,
en la amanecida en el cajón
          con el río para despertarnos.

## [I already recognize myself]

I already recognize myself
in the streets of Santiago
in the overwhelmingly contradictory nature
        of its blood,
certainly in its rebellion
        and its graffitied walls,
in the unforgivable speed
        of its buses,
in its ransacked
        or burned-down corners,
in its icy mornings
        and *merkén*.
I believe in Santiago
like I believe in myself,
        beast born
of indignity. I believe
in its thrushes, in
the *tiuque*'s caw
        resounding of summer,
in the canyon's dawn
        with the river to wake us.

## [¿qué es esto de extrañar el miedo?]

¿qué es esto de extrañar el miedo?

¿de encontrar frías las noches de un verano a medias?

¿qué extraño del miedo?

y me respondo:                la pertenencia

la huella        la marca        aquí bajo mi axila
el miedo        me hizo / el miedo      miradas de óxido

sueño con persecuciones      y falso plomo

[la montaña completaba el escenario]

aquí los montes           no me pertenecen

# [what's this about missing fear?]

what's this about missing fear?

of finding it cold in a half-summer's night?

what do I miss about fear?

I respond:                    the feeling I belong

the footprint      the mark      here beneath my arm
fear                made me / this fear        a gaze of rust

I dream I'm hunted        and I dream of false lead

[the mountain completed the scene]

here the hills        don't belong to me

## [Hemos sido vedados]

Hemos sido vedados
de lo real, de toda apertura.
Se nos ha impedido
el reflejo; nos han puesto
frente a un falso espejo
y se nos dijo:
es esta tu verdad.
Se nos ha cerrado la apertura
de la palabra, cegada
de tantas mentiras que encarna.
Somos los hijos
de la raza enferma,
del útero podrido
de las falacias del Caribe.
Nos han deshecho
las trenzas que nos atan
a los árboles,
luz que atraviesa
todas las pieles
de este valle.
Se nos ha llamado
a las periferias, a los márgenes,
a las tierras ajenas,
donde nuestro nombre
es sombra del vacío
y nada más.

## [Our reality has been banned]

Our reality has been banned,
every opening blocked.
We've been barred
from reflecting; they've placed us
before a false mirror
where we were told:
this is your truth.
The word's aperture
has been closed to us, blinded
by the many lies it embodies.
We're the children
of a sick race,
from the rotten uterus
of the Caribbean's fallacies.
They have undone
the braids that bind us
to the trees,
light which pierces
all of the skin
in this valley.
We've been called
to the peripheries, to the margins,
to other people's lands,
where our name
is emptiness's shadow
and nothing more.

# [¿Qué haremos con el hallazgo?]

¿Qué haremos con el hallazgo,
con el salitre que arranca los pellejos
negros de las rejas que nos enjaulan?

¿Qué haremos
sino coronarlo con sangre?

Degollaremos el hallazgo
desde la cumbre más alta
para sepultar
nuestro valle.

[What will we do with our discovery?]

What will we do with our discovery,
with the saltpeter that rips out
the black bars that cage us?

What will we do
but crown it with blood?

We will slit our discovery's throat
from the highest peak
to bury
our valley.

## [cuando bajé a los infiernos]

cuando bajé a los infiernos
me encontré en mi antigua habitación
con las ventanas abiertas
con las paredes manchadas de mi ausencia
y vi allí los reflejos de la montaña de fuego
las huellas de las mariposas que se posaron
sobre mi almohada sobre mi cama
buscándome    ahora he regresado
y ya no hay nadie ni nada que me aguarde

[when I descended to hell]


when I descended to hell
I found myself in my childhood bedroom
with the windows open
with walls stained by my absence
and there I saw the reflections of the mountain of fire
the tracks of butterflies that lighted
on my pillow on my bed
searching for me      I've returned now
where nobody and nothing awaits me

## [Y así la ciudad que dejé atrás se expande como un cáncer]

Y así la ciudad que dejé atrás se expande como un cáncer invadiendo las geografías que intento habitar desde el desatino / desde la no pertenencia // ciudad que me corroe aún en huida desde el pálpito de lo propio hasta la laguna ajena en los humedales del norte / desplazamiento del dolor de un lado a otro del pecho / sin lugar el corazón de óxido retorcido hacia la garganta deshecha del humo / olvido las calles que no me olvidarán / [calles rotas] calles desperdiciadas en la ebriedad de la miseria de la deriva a cuestas [calles que comienzan a expandirse buscando mi cuerpo] / queriendo cercarme / siendo laberinto egoísta que me alcanza como un pulpo sin tinta / como la incompletitud que me arma lejos / insuficiencia que me desarma ante el claustro de la tierra que me persigue [que me traga] que me quiebra porque no quiere sino abarcar mi propia jaula //

*(Miami, 23/09/2017)*

## [And so the city I left behind expands like cancer]

And so the city I left behind expands like cancer to invade the geographies I try to inhabit from the mistake / from not belonging // city corrodes me still fleeing from its palpitation to the foreign lake in the northern wetlands / pain displaced from one side of the chest to the other / without a place the heart of rust twisted toward a throat unmade by smoke / I forget streets that won't forget me / [broken streets] streets wasted in the intoxication of drifting misery [streets that begin to expand in search of my body] / wanting to enclose me / selfish labyrinth that reaches for me like an inkless octopus / like the incompleteness that arms me afar / insufficiency that disarms me before the earth's cloister following me [swallowing me] which breaks me for it wants nothing but to engulf my cage //

*(Miami, 9/23/2017)*

FERNANDO VANEGAS

## Un hogar entre las piedras

En este poema fuimos felices
Jesús, Josué, Daniel y yo,
mi segunda novia y mi mejor infancia
se dejaron tocar por estos dedos.
Mi primera borrachera
y el primer viaje marihuano me abrazaron
desde atrás cuando todavía me olían las manos
a inocencia.
Aquí encontraron espacio las lágrimas más amargas
que nadie vio jamás
porque yo no lloraba nunca.
Se rompió en este poema
la duda de a dónde diablos iba cargando con
tanto sin darme cuenta,
aquí existió un infierno del que nunca supe
por estar siempre de rumba,
de aquí se escapó el cielo cuando
conoció nuestra tristeza.
Nosotros los tristes,
los amantes,
los niños gritones.
Nosotros los amigos que se besan entre
rincones y luces,
nosotros los dulces mediocres,
los viajeros,
nosotros los de la noche
bañados de sudor de tanto reír y reír
como si las estrellas no estuvieran ya lejos.
Nosotros la memoria de los mismos poemas
que miramos con odio.
Nosotros bailarines de todas las canciones
que se han tocado en esta tierra.

## A Home among the Stones

In this poem we were happy,
Jesús, Josué, Daniel, and I,
my second girlfriend and my childhood best friend
let themselves be touched by these fingers.
The first time I got drunk
and high, they hugged me
from behind when my hands
still smelled of innocence.
Here the bitterest tears found a space
that nobody ever saw
because I never cried.
In this poem the question broke:
where the hell did I go
loaded down by so much without realizing?
Here is a hell I never recognized
in this endless party.
From here, the sky escaped when
it saw our sorrow.
We the sorrowful,
the lovers,
the screaming children.
We the friends who kiss between
dark corners and streetlights,
we the sweetly mediocre,
the travelers,
we of the night
bathed in the sweat of so much laughter
as if the stars were not already so distant.
We the memory of the same poems
that we once read with hatred.
We who danced to all the songs
that have played in this land.

Nosotros los cantantes de media noche,
parados en la calle, temblando de frío,
extrañando a nuestras madres.

Oiga, oiga bien lo que le digo,
no sé nada de dioses,

pero mis amigos deben ser alguno,
mis noches deben ser inmortales,
mi dolor debe ser celestial incluso cuando me tumba
y me patea, cuando me hace escupir barro
y escribir con odio.

Venga, por favor, y abra esta botella
para que se espanten los fantasmas del mundo.
Venga, por favor, y ayúdeme a salir de esta amargura
que me tiene cogido desde hace tanto.
Venga, por favor, y dígame que me ha entendido,
que en lo más hondo del corazón algo le dice
que aún hay ternura.

Dígame que son dulces mis ojos cuando miro
los árboles, que el cabello tan largo debe significar algo,
que seré un hombre viejo cuando acabe esta fiesta.
Dígame que el mar está al otro lado de esa montaña
y que si quiero marcharme el camino vendrá conmigo.

Dígame qué sabe usted del amor,
cuántas veces se ha perdido en la madrugada,
cómo sonríen sus amigos cuando nadie los mira.

Dígame algo, por favor, algo que me ayude a largarme de este
poema donde están todos los que alguna vez me quitaron vida
y me llenaron la mirada de alegría,
los que cambiaron de orden mis pasos
compartiendo conmigo la cerveza,
el ron, el pan, la cama y la sangre.

We who sang at midnight
standing in the street, trembling with cold,
missing our mothers.

Listen, listen well to what I say,
I know nothing of gods,

but my friends must be one of them,
my nights must be immortal,
my pain must be heavenly even when it knocks me down
and kicks me, when it makes me spit mud
and write with hatred.

Come, please, and open this bottle
to scare off the ghosts of the world.
Come, please, and help me leave this bitterness
that has held me for so long.
Come, please, and tell me that you understand me,
that from the heart's depths, something says
there is still tenderness here.

Tell me that my eyes are sweet when I look
at the trees, that my long hair must mean something,
that I will be an old man when this party ends.
Tell me that the sea is on the other side of this mountain
and that if I wanted to leave these streets you'd come with me.

Tell me that you know of love,
of how many times it has been lost at dawn,
of how your friends smile when nobody looks.

Tell me anything, please, anything which helps me to split from this
poem where everything that ever consumed my life
and filled me with a look of joy dwells,
which scrambled my steps
sharing beer, rum,
bread, beds, and blood.

Los que me abrazaron hace años.
Oiga, escuche bien lo que le digo, en este poema
estamos juntos, la vida, el dolor y yo.

———

Estas historias
no son historias todavía,
son lo que espera al otro lado de la ventana.
Esto que tengo en las manos
que se parece tanto a la tristeza
no es una palabra muerta de frío, es el día
que nos cuenta cómo termina todo.
No es el pasado,
es lo que va sucediendo
entre las manos de las mujeres
y las marcas de mis palabras,
es lo que alguna vez dije y me dijeron
para calmar la sed.
Este sonar de campanas, esta herida de bala,
este amigo muerto, esta pierna rota,
todavía no son un poema,
pero ya duelen, ya brillan en el cielo.

———

He brillado hasta caer dormido
queriendo conocer lo claro de la luna.
Dibujé un hogar entre las piedras
para no tener que marcharme otra vez.
Hoy no hay más que la verdad de mis huesos,
la verdad de las palabras tan necesarias como el agua.
He sido
y mi historia la conté hace tiempo.

Those who hugged me years ago.
Listen, listen well to what I say, in this poem
we are together: life, pain, and I.


~


These stories
are not yet stories,
they are what waits on the other side of the window.
What I hold in my hands,
which seems so sad,
isn't a frozen to death word, it's the day
that tells us how everything ends.
It's not the past,
it's what happens
between the hands of women
and the markings of my words,
it's all I've ever told them and been told
to calm my thirst.
This sound of bells, this gunshot wound,
this dead friend, this broken leg,
are not yet a poem,
but they already hurt, already shine in the sky.


~


I shined until falling asleep
wanting to know clear moonlight.
I drew a home among the stones
so I wouldn't have to leave again.
Today there is nothing but the truth of my bones,
the truth of words as necessary as water.
I have been
and I told my story long ago.

Que no me hable del infierno quien no ha visto su nombre acompañado por navajas, quien no ha volteado a mirar a un visitante como si fuera la muerte misma, quien ha caído dormido abrazado por los últimos rayos de los postes. Que no me hable del infierno quien no se ha perdido entre una tristeza infinita y ajena, quien ha perdido su propia tristeza y cuando escribe no se encuentra entre las líneas. Que no me hable del infierno quien siga con vida, que no me hable del infierno quien conoce la calma, que no me hable del infierno quien no reconoce el asco en las alargadas caras de la familia, quien no ha cruzado la mirada con la vergüenza y el miedo. Que no me hable del infierno quien ha estado en él, porque el fuego no es el mismo. Que no me hable del infierno quien tiene el tiempo dividido en horas perfectas, que no me hable del infierno quien llega siempre a tiempo. Que no me hable del infierno quien no se ha descubierto en medio del amanecer con la memoria intacta y los bolsillos vacíos. Que no lo haga, que no me hable del infierno quien no tenga amigos como mis amigos y los vea desaparecer como yo los veo.

Don't tell me of hell, you who haven't heard your name in the flick of switchblades, you who haven't turned to look at a visitor as if they were death itself, you who haven't fallen asleep embraced by the streetlamps' last light. Don't tell me of hell, you who haven't been lost in an infinite and alien sorrow, you who've lost your own sorrow and can't find it between the lines when you write. Don't tell me of hell, you who keep living, don't tell me of hell, you who know peace, don't tell me of hell, you who don't recognize disgust in your family's long faces, who haven't passed through their gaze with shame and fear. Don't tell me of hell, you who've been there, because the fire isn't the same. Don't tell me of hell, you who've divided time into perfect hours, don't tell me of hell, you who always arrive on time. Don't tell me of hell, you who haven't discovered it in the mid-dawn with your memories in place and pockets empty. Don't do it, don't tell me of hell, since you don't have friends like my friends and watch them disappear like I do.

MAXIMILIANO SOJO

## Apagón

Las personas mayores
¿a qué hora volverán?
Da las seis el ciego Santiago,
y ya está muy oscuro.
—CÉSAR VALLEJO

I

las manos arrugadas de los abuelos
después
de ir y venir cargando bolsitas
después
de lavar a mano
no hay descanso en paz

llega la ceguera
arrastra el paludismo
que migró de la fábula a la ciudad

del día en que se acabó esta patria.

II

es la capa de hollín que curte
a duras penas el engranaje
el viejo abuelo recuerda
            valle viejo del que vino
a parar a este abandono
de la greda a los campos de ripio

hasta los confines de un terreno que pesa

90

# Blackout

> At what hour
> will the oldest people return?
> Six o'clock tolls in blind Santiago
> and it's already very dark.
> —CÉSAR VALLEJO

I

after
coming and going with shopping bags
after
washing by hand
the wrinkled hands of grandparents
cannot rest in peace

blindness arrives
dragging malaria from mythology
back into the city

from the day la Patria died

II

with great effort the layers
of soot harden the gears
the old man remembers
             the valley he came from
to stop this neglect
from the clay to the gravel fields

until the borders of our weary land

la máquina guarda
relojes en sus engranajes
óxido que brota como linfa

mientras se mezclan las nubes con los eclipses
se enmarañan los cables
comen ratones el cobre esmeralda
los circuitos anegados por d    e    s    i    e    r    t    o    s

ya no ruge el corazón de la máquina
se apagó en el conticinio

y nos tragó.

III

permanece detenida *la machine*
sus cuatro puertas holladas
cerradas para siempre
acumulan herrumbre
aceite espeso como plasma

se sueltan al precipicio las gotas de la manguera
la máquina espera que le aflojen las tuercas
los neumáticos lisos como recién nacidos
acumularon tetas a los lados
soplan un suspiro que silba

*el aire de otro aire*

la máquina Chevrolet de 82
acumula una capa de hollín
que dejan las otras máquinas
que resisten
                si es que resistir sigue siendo verbo
y ni que le aspiren las alfombras
o los asientos
ni que le pulan los guardafangos

the machine stores
clocks in its gears
rust that wells up like lymph

as clouds mix with eclipses
the wires tangle
mice eat the emerald copper
circuits flooded by d    e    s    e    r    t    s

the machine's heart no longer roars
its howl swallowed us in the dead of night

then blacked out.

III

the machine remains there
its four riddled doors
shut forever
accruing rust
its oil thick as plasma

drops from the hose drip down the cliff
the machine waits for the bolts to loosen
the tires smooth as newborns
amassed tits on their sides
they blow a whistling sigh

                    *air from another air*

the machine is an '82 Chevrolet
that accumulates a layer of soot
left by the other machines
that resist
            if *resist* is still a verb
but they don't vacuum the carpets
nor the seats
nor do they polish the mudguard

ni que te subas con tus viejos lentes de aviador
y apoyes el brazo en la ventana

la máquina tose pero no arranca

ya solo restos de partes dejaron los rateros

       y la gran mancha en el suelo
de las gotas de aceite
que buscando mejor vida
al fondo del precipicio decidieron

                         irse.

nor do you climb in with your old aviator glasses
and rest your arm out the window
the machine coughs but doesn't start

all that remains are the parts spared by thieves

        and a great stain on the soil
from the drops of oil that
searching for a better life
at the bottom of the cliff decided

                to leave.

## Billy

billy solo supo del boom de la pistola
no supo de física
ni de las vueltas del boomerang
no le dio tiempo
supo del boom como los otros
por aquella pistolita que le regaló su padre en carnaval
no supo del boom latinoamericano
billy supo del boom cuando los proyectiles percutían
reventando fémures cadera esternón
billy no supo que todo lo que sube baja
prefirió agujerear las zonas blandas de los carajitos en la cancha
no supo de newton
ni por crecer junto a mi casa
ni por morir frente a su madre
ni la glock 9 mm
ni sangrando por cabeza, tronco y extremidades.

## Billy

billy only knew the pistol's boom
but nothing of physics
or the boomerang's return
he was out of time
like everyone else he knew the boom
in the pistol his father gave him at carnival
but not the latin american boom
billy knew the boom when bullets hit
bursting femurs hips and sternums
but billy didn't know the third law
he preferred to puncture the smooth bellies of kids on the court
he didn't know of newton
of dying in front of his mother
of the 9 mm glock
of growing up next door to me
of bleeding out his head and torso and extremities.

## Missvenezuela

buenas noches, poliedro

a la derecha la muerta

la violada
tirada a un costado del alfoz

la que se perdió sin pasaporte
se operó las tetas en oferta
con el cupo cadivi
por pundonor

miss [muerta en el extranjero]
un fuerte aplauso.

## Missvenezuela

good evening, Caracas

on your right, the dead woman

raped
tossed on the side of a country road

lost without her passport,
budget boob job
with her CADIVI allowance,
out of self-respect

miss [dead abroad]
a round of applause.

## Que la palabra diga

que la palabra diga
que el tiro calle la boca del muerto
no la nuestra
ni la de ellos
que la palabra sea saliva ardiente
el escupo en la palabra del muerto
no la nuestra ni la de ellos
la tuya abierta como puertas para moscas
secreta
el líquido que suena
que cambia el mundo
desde la garganta
hasta los tímpanos temerosos
del tirano
que ronca
que suelta el tiro en tu palabra
y en la nuestra y en la de ellos
que casi gana
está a punto de silenciar
los puentes en las caries
que tu palabra se alce más que tú

                    tú no eres nada sin tu palabra
                    no eres nada sin tu palabra
                    no eres nada sin tu palabra

eres tu palabra alzada más que tú
más que la torre
más que nosotros y más que ellos
que no se alzan
que se aburren
que se venden
que se compran
que se llevan a la tumba
como el muerto
que ni silbó

## Let the Word Be Spoken

let the word be spoken
let the gunshot silence only death's mouth
but not ours
and not the mouths of others
let the word be burning saliva
and let it spit on death's word
but not our words or the words of others
your mouth opens like a door for flies
secreting
that resounding liquid
that changes the world
and pours from the throat
until it reaches tyranny's
terrifying timpani
which roar
and fire shots at your word
and at our words and at the words of others
tyranny nearly wins
it's on the point of silencing
the bridges along the cavities and teeth
that raise your word higher than you

                    you are nothing without your word
                    nothing without your word
                    nothing without your word

you are a word raised higher than yourself
higher than a tower
higher than us and higher than them
higher than those who don't raise themselves
higher than those who grow bored
higher than those who sell themselves out
or those who buy what they're selling
higher than those who deliver themselves to the grave
like the dead
who do not whistle

que si te callas
tu silencio sea alquitrán
que rompa el cartílago
que seque la lengua
que el maxilar explote
y las muelas
que deje la tráquea rota
y te ahogues
porque el que se calla

es cómplice

and if you fall silent
let your silence be tar
that breaks your cartilage
and dries your tongue
shattering
your molars and your jaw
breaking your trachea
and you choke
because he who stays silent

is complicit

## Córtex

se abren mis ventanas y mis escombros
yo también soy el oleaje
sueño con no volver
aunque vuelva
la piedrita en el zapato
de mi calle llena de barro
las escaleras
porque otra vez se fue la luz
y ni siquiera el piso lustrado brilla
ni chirría
y no hay zapatos ni suelas
ni fuerza para dar el paso
o para subir al quinto piso o al sexto
y lanzarse
de cabeza sobre el asfalto
abrir otro hueco olor a cráneo chamuscado
quedar con el cuerpo laxo
a la salida
que de noche
la sangre también es petróleo
por excavar
si la cabeza fuera más dura
perforaría un hoyo profundo
más profundo
llegaría a la corteza
al crack
inmediato de la duramadre
tierra
que resistes no sé por qué
tierra
que puedes morirte y
tierra
no te mueres.

## Cortex

my windows and my ruins open
I too am the sea swell
I dream of not going back
although a pebble
in a shoe does come back
from my mud-filled street
taking the stairs
because the power's out again
and not even the polished floor squeaks
or shines
and there are no shoes or soles
no strength to take a step
or to go up to the fifth or sixth floor
and jump headfirst
down to the concrete
cracking another hole the smell of burnt skull
hovering around the slack body
at the exit
and at night
blood is also oil
to be drilled for
if that skull were harder
it would pierce a deep hole
the deepest hole
it would reach the earth's cortex
to the crack
adjoining its dura mater
my land
you bear it all but I don't know why
my land
you could drop dead but
my land
you do not die.

## Padre

cuando lo conocí
a los trece años
tuve miedo
del soldado
que me abortó
a quien las botas habían torcido
los dedos de los pies
tuve miedo
de que se arrepintiera
me arrojara sus disculpas
como hacen los soldados
que preparan una guerra
a la que nunca irán
frustrados
dejan dos o tres mensajes
que yo veo y no respondo
hasta que me entero
de que ha muerto
y que he abortado un padre

## Father

when I met him
at thirteen
I was scared
of the soldier
who aborted me
whose boots had warped
his toes
I was scared
he'd come to regret it
that he'd spew his apologies at me
like soldiers
getting ready for a war
they'll never go to
frustrated they leave me
two or three messages
that I see but don't respond to
until I hear about
who has died
and that I've aborted a father

## Malamuerte

al papá de mi padrastro lo encontraron
muerto en el centro el tórax abierto
en la cama destendida de un hotel
de mala muerte
por algo mala muerte tuvo el viejo
macho calvo callejero

el hotel no tiene culpa de la mala
muerte del viejo
la mala vida
que sacó hijos de sus testículos, de su calvicie

muerto el viejo en un hotel de mala muerte
en el centro de Caracas
muerto de mala muerte el viejo calvo
infartado
desnudo y lánguido
abierto en el centro de la cama

su hijo mayor
el imitador
heredó los testículos llenos de nata
los pelos en el pecho
la calvicie
la suerte de la muerte mala
en el centro de la cama
solo
millonario en bolívares devaluados

al padre de mi padrastro lo mató el morbo
se casó con el ron que le hinchó los cachetes
lo encontraron verde
y su primogénito

## Motel Malamuerte

they found my stepfather's father downtown,
dead in a fleabag motel
in an unmade bed
his chest burst open
by the bad life that old
bald bum had lived

the motel wasn't guilty
of that old man's bad death
a bad life
had siphoned children from his balls, from his baldness

the old man died in a shitty motel
in the middle of Caracas
and it was a bad death
a heart attack
naked and lifeless
opened up in the middle of the bed

his oldest son
looked up to him
he inherited his bloated balls
his hairy chest
his baldness
and the luck of a bad death
alone
in the middle of the bed
a millionaire in worthless bolivars

these desires killed my stepfather's father
he'd married the rum that bloated his cheeks
he was green when they found him
and now his firstborn

babosea en su nombre
mientras se abarrota los genitales
con espuma.

slobbers in his name
as his genitals
foam.

MIGUEL A. HERNÁNDEZ ZAMBRANO

# Los niños del 83

Aquí están tus niños del 83. Ellos no saben de generaciones, pero serán una. Cuando crecieron se les cayó el ánimo y patearon los patios de la infancia. Y ya no los consiguen en sus casas ni caminando en el *mall* (es muy obvio); hay que revisar sus nombres en Internet, solicitarlos, esperarlos. Lo sentimos, viejo lago, nunca conocimos esas aguas; lo sentimos, Semana de la Zulianidad, no sabemos de semanas ni de zulianidad, crecimos sin pasado y sin ciudad. ¿Qué pasó ayer? No se puede saber, no hay forma . . . y no importa y nadie se acuerda.

No tienen rabia, ellos apenas están ahí. De vez en cuando se toman un par de cervezas y se excitan con las vecinas que ven salir una que otra ocasión.

Fuera de eso no hay mucho más.

Nuestros padres hablaron de un tiempo heroico en que levantaron edificios, museos, calles, grandes avenidas, plazas románticas y brindaban con petróleo destilado. Pero para ellos esas fueron las historias con que los dormían. Insistimos: no hay forma de saber cómo sucedieron las cosas. Por eso acuden al diccionario cuando en la televisión escuchan la palabra *terruño*. ¿A qué se refiere?

¿De qué hablan en la TV? ¿Qué dicen en la radio? ¿Qué significa lo que salió en el periódico de hoy? Es el más reciente capítulo de la telenovela, la opera non plus ultra de Venevisión Plus, de VTV, de CNN, de Globovisión, de ESPN, de Disney Channel, de Tlnovelas, de Pasiones, de TCM, de Discovery, de ANTV, de MTV, de VH1, de E! Entertainment Television . . . los buenos y los malos, *fantasías animadas de ayer y hoy* . . . [El *zapping* les dijo cómo escribir poemas]

A ver si nos entendemos. Ellos no quieren romper con la tradición, simplemente no tienen tradición. ¿No la tienen? *Nada que ver, abuela, la moda* . . .

Pero insisten como si ellos tuvieran memoria, como si hablaran el mismo idioma. Ellos saben que la autopista está lenta y que el CD se les quedó en el cuarto; por suerte el aire del carro enfría bien. No pidan más. O vayan a cantar himnos y cantos

# The Children of '83

Here we are, your children of '83. We don't know about generations, but we'll be one. Once grown, we lost our spirit and kicked the dust of our childhood playgrounds. And now we can't be found in our houses or hanging out in malls (too obvious); you must check our names online, solicit us, wait for us. Sorry, old lake, we never knew those waters; sorry Week of the Zulianidad, we didn't know of weeks or of Zulianidad, we grew up without a past and without a city. What happened yesterday? There's no telling . . . there's no way . . . and it doesn't matter and nobody remembers.

We aren't angry, we're barely there. Once in a while, we have a few beers and get excited when we glimpse the girls next door going out.

Not much more other than that.

Our parents spoke of a heroic time when they raised buildings, museums, streets, grand avenues, and romantic plazas, toasting each other with distilled oil. But for us, those were our bedtime stories. We insisted: there's no way to tell how things happened. That's why we turn to the dictionary when we hear the word *Patria*. What's that mean?

What are they talking about on TV? What are they saying on the radio? The things published in today's newspaper, what do they mean? It's the telenovela's newest episode, the non plus ultra opera from Venevision Plus, from VTV, from CNN, from Globovisión, from ESPN, from the Disney Channel, from Tlnovelas, from Pasiones, from TCM, from Discovery, from ANTV, from MTV, from VH1, from E! Entertainment Television . . . the good ones and the bad ones, *animated fantasies of yesterday and today* . . . [channel surfing taught them how to write poems]

Let's see if we understand each other. It's not that we want to break with tradition, we simply don't have tradition. We don't have it? *Nada que ver, abuela, la moda* . . .

de alabanza en el centro, mientras que los niños del 83 se meten en el apartamento y dejan correr completo el *playlist* del iPod a todo volumen y beben y se besan con niñas del 84 en la sala hasta que se duermen con el TV encendido, una película del 95 que nadie recuerda y la imagen de las vecinas bajo la almohada.

But they insist as if they remember, as if they speak the same language. They know the highway is backed up and that they left their CDs in their room; fortunately, the car's air conditioning works. Don't ask for more. Or go downtown to sing anthems and songs of praise, while the children of '83 go into the apartment and play entire playlists on their iPod at full volume and drink and kiss girls from '84 in the living room until we fall asleep with the TV on, some film from '95 that nobody remembers and an image of the girls next door under our pillow.

## Todo estaba bien:

había cervezas de todos los colores, whiskey destilado magistralmente, mujeres que susurraban mi nombre, comida abundante, playas cercanas, compartíamos poemas al margen de las fiestas y la noche acogía nuestras caminatas y nuestro cansancio.

Todo estaba bien, aunque fuera una mentira, aunque estuviera marcado por la ingenuidad y el miedo.

Todo estaba bien
hasta que dejó de estarlo.

Desde entonces odio el verano.

## All Was Good:

there was beer of every color, masterfully distilled whiskey, women who whispered my name, abundant food, nearby beaches, we shared poems on the edges of parties and the night welcomed our rambles and our fatigue.

All was good, even though it was a lie, even though it was marked by naïveté and fear.

All was good
until it wasn't.

And ever since, I've hated summer.

## Supercrown cerró

Supercrown cerró, Routine cerró, Blind Barber cerró (en Lorimer St.), Hops & Hocks cerró, Covert cerró, Secret Project Robot lo hará en dos semanas, The Undercover Dream Lovers se mudó a Los Ángeles, Josephine regresó a Baltimore, Krista se fue a Georgia, Liz ya no está en Variety, Luisa volvió a Oporto, Alana abrió su barbería en Greenpoint, Kyle se fue a Clinton Hill, Joe se fue a Ridgewood, Courtney solo me regaló algo de psicodelia turca, Astoria cambió de ecosistema el verano de 2017 y la verdad es que nadie sabe qué hacer con la línea L.

Al final, toda mi energía se iba en recorrer zonas industriales con ventanas hechas pedazos y cielos grises a pesar del verano, ver bandas en pequeños bares, intentar reunirme con los pocos amigos y rebotar sin control entre Left Hand Path, The Three Diamond Door, Molasses y Birdy's.

La ciudad me lo advertía: vete.

Sin saberlo ya era parte de una nueva mudanza.

## Supercrown Closed

Supercrown closed, Routine closed, Blind Barber (on Lorimer St.) closed, Hops & Hocks closed, Covert closed, Secret Project Robot will shut down in two weeks, The Undercover Dream Lovers moved to Los Angeles, Josephine went back to Baltimore, Krista moved to Georgia, Liz doesn't work at *Variety* anymore, Luisa returned to Oporto, Alana opened up her barbershop in Greenpoint, Kyle went to Clinton Hill, Joe went to Ridgewood, Courtney just gave me some Turkish psychedelia, Astoria's ecosystem changed in the summer of 2017, and the truth is nobody knows what to do with the L train.

In the end, all my energy went toward wandering through industrial zones with shattered windows and with gray skies despite it being summer, seeing bands in dive bars, trying to meet up with my few remaining friends, bouncing uncontrollably between the Left Hand Path, the Three Diamond Door, Molasses, and Birdy's.

The city warned me: go away.

Without knowing it, I was already part of another move.

## [La avenida]

La avenida
todo parece normal

*Disculpe. ¡Trabajamos para usted!*

una mentada de madre
el camino de tierra

ejercicio Hänsel-y-Gretel
para volver.

## [The avenue]

The avenue
everything seems normal

*Excuse us. We work for you!*

someone yells *motherfucker*
down the dirt road

Hansel-and-Gretel exercise
to return.

[Había en aquellos viejos libros infantiles otro país particularmente extraño.]

(Había en aquellos viejos libros infantiles otro país particularmente extraño. Al parecer se llamaba Chile, pero los registros no coinciden. A veces escrito también Shile, $hile o $h¥ı€, entre otros muchos nombres. El lenguaje desapareció ahí mucho antes de mi nacimiento. Se dice que quedaban grupos antiguos, de otras galaxias, que atinaban sonidos heredados de las piedras. Lo primero en desaparecer fueron las vocales, que pronto reemplazaron algunas consonantes como la x. Para entonces ya el agua alcanzaba hasta la garganta de los moradores de esos valles y desiertos. Después vino la pérdida de comunicación. Llegaron habitantes de diferentes planetas, incluso de otras galaxias. Cada quien hacía sonidos distintos y aplaudía por cosas diversas. La Tierra se llenó de extraterrestres con sus gorjeos y zumbidos especiales, por lo que no hubo forma de legislar sobre esa parte in-hóspita del planeta. Sin posibilidad alguna de comunicación, las palabras antiguas, heredadas de otros imperios, se fueron dejando de usar poco a poco, hasta que un día una madre no pudo darle los buenos días a la hija y, sin más, con una mueca triste, ambas entendieron que todo había terminado.)

[In those old children's books there was another strange country.]


(In those old children's books there was another strange country. It was said to be called "Chile," but the records differ. Sometimes its name was written as Shile, $hile, or $h¥ı€, among many others. The language there disappeared long before my birth. Ancient groups from other galaxies are said to remain, who discovered sounds inherited from the stones. The vowels were the first to disappear, soon replaced by consonants such as *x*. By then, the water had already reached the throats of those who inhabited those valleys and deserts. Then came the loss of communication. Residents from other planets and galaxies arrived. Each made different sounds and applauded different things. The land filled with extraterrestrials, each with their own peculiar chirp or buzz, and so legislating over that inhospitable part of the planet became impossible. With no way to communicate, the ancient words, inherited from other empires, were abandoned bit by bit, until one day a mother couldn't say good morning to her daughter, and with a sad grin, both understood that everything was over.)

# [Antes de que perdiéramos toda comunicación]

Antes de que perdiéramos toda comunicación
Felipe dijo que seríamos como piedras
Ignacia, que de alguna forma tendríamos un lenguaje
        y luego habló del Apocalipsis

pero eso fue hace mucho tiempo
y no sabría cómo referirme a esa época
solo que para entonces aún decíamos cosas
        torpemente

haciendo gestos exagerados como ensayando un nuevo idioma
y jugábamos juegos de mesa
y comíamos pizza como si hubiera un mañana que pudiéramos imaginar

pero estaba lejos de nuestras palabras
y más allá de eso
éramos niños girando en un columpio desvencijado
repitiendo una sola sílaba
buscando el punto en que la saliva encuentra nuevos colores y nuevos sabores
sílabas como ti
como ra
como fe
como ma
como pe
hasta que la mecánica de la lujuria nos hacía caer en el pasto seco
        para buscarnos y tocarnos unos a otros
como piedras llenas de cargas eléctricas
imposibles de acomodar sobre un escritorio

así fue como llegamos al fin del tiempo
un día que temblamos más de la cuenta
y perdimos los últimos vestigios de palabras
        que brotaban de los dientes.

## [Before we lost all communication]


Before we lost all communication
Felipe said we'd be like stones
and Ignacia said we'd still have a language somehow
        and then she talked about the Apocalypse

but that was long ago
and I didn't know how I'd later think of that era
it's just that back then we still said things
        awkwardly

making exaggerated gestures as if teaching a new language
and we played board games
and we ate pizza as if there were a tomorrow we could imagine

but I was far away from our words
and beyond that
we were kids swinging on a rickety swing set
repeating a single syllable
looking for the point where our spit would find new colors and new flavors
syllables like *ti*
like *ra*
like *fe*
like *ma*
like *pe*
until the mechanics of lust made us fall to the dry grass
        to look for each other and touch each other
like stones full of electric charges
impossible to fit on a desk

and so we arrived at the end of time
a day where we trembled too much
and lost the last traces of the words
        that once sprouted from our teeth.

## [Ya no sabíamos cómo hablar]

Ya no sabíamos cómo hablar
y hacía tiempo que vivíamos alejados unos de otros
cuando hubo necesidad de salir
nadie confiaba en nadie
y nos mirábamos de reojo
o nos cambiábamos de acera para evitarnos

las pocas personas que se tropezaban
despedían un sonido metálico que nos ponía nerviosos

habíamos dormido un largo sueño
y ahora damos tumbos
recién nacidos que se abisman por primera vez al patio de la calle
ansiosos y temblorosos
nos mordemos los dedos
y miramos el sol con sospecha
—demasiado fuego para los nuevos metales oxidados que empezamos a ser—
ya no sabemos cómo buscar comida o bajar las escaleras
no hay forma
todo quedó en la memoria de un cuerpo antiguo
blando y frágil
acostumbrado al sexo y a bebidas hechas para la desmesura
por eso estábamos enfermos y tristes
por eso seguimos enfermos y tristes
pero con órganos renovados que solo podrán soportar nuestra ruina unos pocos años
hasta que vean cómo nos masticamos unos a otros
puro balbuceo
puro grito hundido en la garganta
saliva demoledora
saliva máquina de desechos
huesos de miedo
pieles ansiosas que fueron dejando atrás las compras diarias
las 900 notificaciones de los viejos teléfonos
el paseo del GPS

## [We didn't know how to speak anymore]


We didn't know how to speak anymore
we'd lived disconnected from one another for a long time
when there was a need to go out
nobody trusted anyone
and we shot each other sideways glances
or we crossed the street

the few people we ran into
gave off metallic sounds that made us nervous

we'd dreamt a long dream
and now we stumble
newborns become inconsolable their first time outside
anxious and trembling
we bite our knuckles
and we behold the sun with suspicion
—too much fire for this rusty new metal we're becoming—
we don't know how to look for food or go down the stairs
there's no form
everything was left in an elderly body's memory
soft and fragile
used to sex and heavy drinking
this is why we were sick and sad
this is why we're still sick and sad
but with updated organs that can bear our ruin only a few years
until they see how we chew each other up
only babble
only a scream sinking in a throat
demolition saliva
saliva debris machine
fear bones
anxious skins that daily errands left behind
the nine hundred notifications on the old iPhone
the GPS walk

las vibraciones de la pierna
los músculos de silicio
el hambre fantasma del falso estómago
el deseo imposible de quien nunca ha existido
y todo lo que creímos que nos salvaría finalmente del silencio
     y de la recién estrenada soledad.

the vibrations on the leg
the silicone muscles
the false stomach's phantom hunger
the impossible longing for someone who never existed
and everything we thought would finally save us from silence
        and from this newly released solitude.

GLADYS MENDÍA

## Mundo

nuestro mundo son las voces    hablan tan fuerte que es imposible no escucharlas    nuestra diversidad asusta    quieren que seamos una masa    que hablemos igual    que escribamos igual    las voces guaraníes son una amenaza al neoliberalismo    las voces mapuches son bombas a punto de explotar            las voces mayas son un acto de subversión            las voces wayúu son disparos al sistema    las voces quechua son misiles explotando las instituciones nuestra diversidad es un atentado            camino por las calles de mi barrio y los represores han hecho un excelente trabajo masificados todos uniformados todos            anestesiados todos cosificados en el tránsito siguiendo la señalética acelerando en las autopistas estrellados sin luz    soñando con la desobediencia

# World

our world of voices      speaks so strongly that it's impossible not to
listen     our diversity frightens    they want us to be a mass     speaking
the same    writing the same    Guaranie voices threaten neoliberalism
Mapuche voices are bombs ready to explode      Mayan voices are an
act of subversion            Wayuu voices fire shots into the system
Quechua voices are missiles exploding institutions    our diversity is
an attack      I walk through my neighborhood and see the repressors
have done excellent work    overcrowding us      homogenizing us
anesthetizing us       everything reified in transit following the signs
speeding down the freeway       starry but without light    dreaming
of disobedience

## antes de la caída la levedad del vidrio

el vidrio estalla en la boca       sus minúsculas
partes flotando     la lengua una minúscula parte
las ondas de letras suspendidas    tal vez la voz
sea sentirnos

no hay direcciones     los mapas no sirven en las trans-
parencias   sin puntos de referencia soñamos viajar tal vez
llegamos a decirnos algo      tal vez no

del vidrio se puede ver el filo    algo azulado    algo de
límite    estalla en silencio como la respiración    el
tiempo son las minúsculas partes soñando que flotan
se creen transparentes    creen que vuelan    pero es
la antesala a la caída

la medida es la tensión     las minúsculas partes arden
entre el flotar y el caer   la tensión con la luz las hacen
brillar    la tensión con el aire las hacen suspenderse

las minúsculas partes son los hormigueos del aire
sus bordes eléctricos titilando   breves heridas que se
estiran en curvas   el ojo asiste   se alarga como astilla
y ve algo

## the lightness of glass before the fall

glass shatters in a mouth            its smallest pieces
floating          the tongue a small piece        the ripples
of these suspended letters      maybe the voice is sensing us

there are no directions            maps don't work on trans-
lucent things      without points of reference we dream of
travel maybe    we'll reach some conclusion about ourselves
maybe not

from the glass one can see the edge        something bluish
some limit      explodes in silence like a breath        like time
the smallest dreaming parts float                  they believe
transparent          they believe they fly        but this is just
an antechamber before the fall

measurement is tension              the smallest pieces burn
between floating and falling      the tension with light makes
them shine                the tension with air suspends them

the smallest pieces are the air's tingling      their electric
edges flicker      brief wounds that stretch        and bend
the eye witnesses      it lengthens like a splinter          and
sees something

# La grita: confusión de voces
Reescritura de *Las moradas* de Teresa de Ávila

Especialmente a mis hijas Érika y Bárbara

A las mujeres de mi familia

La crudeza del mundo era tranquila. El asesinato era profundo.
Y la muerte no era aquello que pensábamos.
—CLARICE LISPECTOR

## PRIMER PELDAÑO
Barahúnda

Veisme aquí, mi dulce Amor,
Amor dulce, veisme aquí,
¿Qué mandáis hacer de mí?
—TERESA DE ÁVILA

esto no puede comenzar así
las palabras son hielos que ruedan por el suelo antes de ser charco
aguas turbias invaden los pasillos
el incendio en sonoro parpadeo muestra el doble reflejo
no les puedo decir lo que pasa
tal vez si las abrazo
si llevo sus oídos a mi pecho

alguien llama
no abran
no espero a nadie
el viento helado
de los charcos asesina
miren cómo estamos con el agua hasta las rodillas
qué haremos con tanta agua
cuiden sus oídos de esos charcos de miedo

estaba tejiendo y se perdieron mis hilos
cuando entraron las primeras gotas al castillo
les conté sobre las aguas turbias

# The Scream: A Confusion of Voices

Rewriting *The Interior Castle,* by Teresa of Avila

> To the women of my family,
>> especially for my daughters, Érika and Bárbara

> The world's roughness was calm. The killing was profound.
> And death was not what we thought.
>> —CLARICE LISPECTOR

## THE FIRST STEP

Bewilderment

> See me here, my sweet Love,
> Sweet Love, see me here,
> What do You will of me?
>> —TERESA OF AVILA

it can't begin like this
my words are ice they roll across the floor then melt
the dark puddles flood the corridors
the fire's heavy flickering reveals a double reflection
I can't tell my daughters what's happening
maybe if I hug them
if I press their ears to my chest

someone is knocking
do not open it
I wait for nobody
the icy wind
of the killing puddles
look how we're up to our knees in water
what will we do with so much water?
protect your ears from those fearful puddles

I was weaving and my threads were lost
when the first drops of water entered the castle
I told my daughters of the dark puddles

que cuando entran no salen
antes fue en el sueño
por eso dije que cerraran la puerta
miraba por encima del hombro hacia atrás
unas luces querían ahogar mis ojos
ahora mis vestidos y zapatos mojados en el castillo donde todos entran

los murciélagos cuelgan del techo
¿escuchan ese sonido?
es como en el sueño
hermanitas
saquen las gotas que me confunden los charcos

camino dormida por los pasillos
subo escalón tras escalón
metálicos murciélagos cuelgan
¿por qué no sacan la pestilencia del castillo?
mis hilos
ahora los recuerdo
estaba tejiendo a la hora de las gotas
unos abrigos para el verano

mis manos
¿dónde dejé mis manos?

hay tiempos donde se vive el mar
como un sueño recurrente
no sé si deba contarlo
ay hijitas
el mar se lleva mis manos
cada dedo en la boca de un pez moribundo

dijeron que estamos en el castillo de gotas
sobre los reflejos del incendio
el castillo doble reflejo
sin patio y sin perro en medio de la autopista

that they flow in but not out
I have dreamed this before
that's why I told them to close the door
I looked back over my shoulder
a few lights wanted to drown my eyes
now my dresses and shoes are wet in a castle where everything enters

bats hang from the ceiling
do they hear that sound?
it's like my dream
oh my sisters
drain the water from these puddles that baffle me

I sleepwalk through the corridors
I climb stair after stair
the metallic bats hang
why don't they expel this plague from the castle?
my threads
I remember them now
in the time of the water
I was weaving summer coats

my hands
where did I leave my hands?

there are times when the sea is lived
like a recurring dream
I don't know if I should recount it
oh my daughters
the sea takes my hands
each finger in the mouth of a dying fish

they said that we're in the castle of water
on the reflections of the fire
the castle's two reflections in the middle of the highway
without a courtyard and without a dog

¿quién llama a la puerta?
no quiero abrir
les dije que no estoy
el incendio deja su huella en los charcos
el doble reflejo intenta cantar toda esta barahúnda

hijitas
los vecinos están de fiesta
se escuchan sus canciones alegres
se escuchan sus pasos de baile
¿les dije que me gusta bailar?
ahora lo recuerdo
eso del sueño recurrente
todo empezaba en la orilla
viendo las olas
una grande venía hacia mí
corría y miraba hacia atrás
la mano del mar me perseguía
todas las noches lo mismo
el sudor helado de la huida

siento un mordisqueo en los talones
con las aguas turbias siempre llegan los peces raros
hoy es viernes
comeremos pescado

hijitas ¿por qué no creo?
¿por qué los brazos caídos?
¿por qué la ausencia de voz?

desde el primer piso se ven las escaleras de arena
no hay pasamanos
no hay extinguidor
hijitas
quería decirles que siempre se sube con la boca seca
y el agua hasta las rodillas

who knocks?
I don't want to open the door
I told them I'm not here
the fire burns its mark across the puddles
the double reflection tries singing all this bewilderment

oh my daughters
the neighbors are partying
they listen to their happy songs
I can hear their dance steps
did I tell them I like dancing?
I remember it now
in my recurring dream
everything began on the shore
watching the waves
a huge one barreled towards me
I ran and I looked back
the ocean's hand chased me
every night is the same
the icy sweat of flight

something gnaws at my heels
strange fish always arrive with the dark waters
today's friday
we'll eat fish

oh my daughters why don't I believe?
why do my arms always drop?
where's my voice?

on the first floor a staircase of sand
with no handrails
and no extinguisher
my daughters
I wanted to tell you that you always ascend it with a dry mouth
and water lapping at your knees

ruedo por el piso en vueltas de canela
conozco bien cada astilla hundiéndose en la espalda
quisiera encontrar el silencio
quisiera
pero no sé

las escaleras solo existen para subir
con la lengua volteada intento correr
pero no logro avanzar
y todo por la prisa

desde aquí puedo ver las puertas
dejamos una abierta
todo está lleno de polvo
todo luce desgastado
hermanitas
quería decirles que si subo un escalón
ustedes suben conmigo

duele el destierro
me duele tanto como lo amo
duelen los charcos que desconozco
no sé si quiera explicarlo más tarde

puedo pasar siglos en un escalón
¿sabían?

hermanas
por debajo de la puerta sale un reflejo luminoso
no sé si es agua o fuego
todo depende de la mano que lo toca

ya escribimos la cordillera
pero no es suficiente
hermanas
los charcos se me caen de las manos

I roll in cinnamon bark across the floor
I intimately know each splinter that sinks into my back
I'd like to find silence
I'd like to
but I don't know how

the stairs can only be climbed
I try to run with a twisted tongue
I don't make progress
and everything's done in haste

from here I can see the doors
we left one open
everything is full of dust
everything looks worn
my sisters
I wanted to tell you that if I climb a step
you climb with me

exile hurts
it hurts me as much as I love it
the puddles that I don't know hurt
I don't know if I should explain it later

I can spend centuries on a step
did they know?

sisters
a radiant reflection escapes from under the door
I don't know if it's water or fire
it all depends on the hand that touches it

we already wrote the mountain range
but it's not enough
sisters
the dark water pours from my hands

veo hojas de árboles como gotas
las veo bajar del cielo sonando río
y son puñales livianos como plumas

estaba pensando en el tiempo de los charcos
es un tiempo muy quieto
parecido al de las rocas

estaba pensando hermanitas en la nieve
los cristales estallando
nosotras cayendo como rosas de hielo sobre los charcos

hay tantos cuartos como latidos
hay tantas ventanas como espejos
el viento se enfurece con las cortinas
los portarretratos
las figuras del armario y caen
caen porque todo cae
finalmente

hay un brillo adentro
hermanas
hay un brillo sin charcos que no se parece a nada

## SEGUNDO PELDAÑO
Turbaciones

> Nada te turbe;
> nada te espante;
> todo se pasa
> —TERESA DE ÁVILA

hermanas
esta náusea no se quita
miro alrededor y nada
de nuevo todo está oscuro

I see the leaves of the trees are droplets
I see them fall from the sky they sound like a river
they are daggers as light as feathers

I was thinking of how time for these puddles
is a motionless time
like that of stones

oh sisters I was thinking of the snow
of the shattering crystals
of us falling like roses of ice across the water

there are as many rooms as heartbeats
there are as many windows as mirrors
the wind becomes infuriated with the curtains
with the picture frames
with the shape of the wardrobe
and they fall
they fall because everything falls eventually

there is a brightness inside
sisters
there is a pure brilliance unlike anything else

### THE SECOND STEP
Troubles

> Nothing troubles you;
> nothing frightens you;
> everything comes to pass
> —TERESA OF AVILA

sisters
there's no relief from this nausea
I look around and nothing
everything is dark again

¿cuándo se acabará esta noche?
¿cuándo llegará el alba?
hermanitas siento mareos de abismo

ayer encontré serpientes
bajando las escaleras
tropecé con ellas
caí
era un hervidero al caer
tapé mis oídos
y escuché una voz

pienso salir del castillo
la voz insiste que no lo haga

esta voz es tan dulce
susurra que deje de andar
por castillos ajenos
que afuera
no hallaré paz

tengo sed
tengo hambre
pero esta sed
y esta hambre
no se quitan
con pan y agua

hijitas
en ocasiones me busco
y no me hallo
ando derramada
como charcos por las escaleras

paz
me dice el dulce susurro
pero ¿cómo?

when will the night end?
when will dawn arrive?
oh sisters I'm dizzy above this abyss

yesterday I found serpents
descending the stairs
I stumbled over them
I fell
I was falling water
I covered my ears
and I heard a voice

I think of leaving this castle
but the voice insists I stay

this voice is so tender
it whispers for me
to stop wandering
to far-off castles
outside I will not find peace

I'm thirsty
I'm hungry
but this thirst
and this hunger
can't be abated
by bread and water

oh my daughters
sometimes I search for myself
but find nothing
I'm spilling
like water down the stairs

*peace*
the sweet voice whispers
but how?

## TERCER PELDAÑO

Combates

> El amor cuando es crecido
> no puede estar sin obrar,
> ni el fuerte sin pelear,
> por amor de su querido
> —TERESA DE ÁVILA

después de mucho subir
apenas el tercer peldaño

hermanitas

no hay nada seguro
cada paso es un salto al vacío
el dulce susurro dice que no suelte las armas
que no se puede dormir ni descansar
una vez que el ascenso ha comenzado

el viento azota las puertas
justo al crepúsculo
son truenos golpeando el pecho

hijitas
¿cuándo terminará este sobresalto?

este perderse muchas veces es harto cansado
este hablar sin decir

la dulce voz susurra *calme la mente*

## THE THIRD STEP
Combat

> For love to reach its height
> it must be by work alone,
> like the strong will always fight
> for their dearest ones
> —TERESA OF AVILA

after so much climbing
only the third step

oh sisters

nothing is certain
each step is a jump into the abyss
the voice whispers *do not drop your weapons*
*you cannot sleep nor rest*
*now that the ascent has begun*

the wind scours the doors
right at dusk
claps of thunder strike my chest

oh my daughters
is there any end to this dread?

I'm so tired of being lost
of speaking but saying nothing

the voice whispers *calm your mind*

## CUARTO PELDAÑO

Entrega

> Veis aquí mi corazón,
> yo le pongo en vuestra palma,
> mi cuerpo, mi vida y alma,
> mis entrañas y afición
> —TERESA DE ÁVILA

en el cuarto peldaño entra un rayo de luz

hermanas
no ha sido fácil llegar
el aire luce transparente

ya no hay murciélagos
ni serpientes
las aguas turbias apenas son un mal recuerdo

antes era todo confuso
estrecho
el pensamiento afuera
el alma apretada
así era la barahúnda
era dos siendo una
padeciendo y mereciendo con este padecer

siento unas manos
vienen en sueños
sus largos dedos buscan el corazón
se detienen a escuchar sus latidos
me acarician
y crean primaveras en estrellas

todo es complaciente dulce y lento
dilataste *cor meum* en cada latido
el castillo crece con esta fuente
emanando emanando emanando

## THE FOURTH STEP
Devotion

> Look here at my heart,
> I place it in Your palm,
> my body, life, and soul,
> my entrails and my qualms
> —TERESA OF AVILA

on the fourth step a beam of light

sisters
arriving here has not been easy
the air translucently shines

there are no more bats
or serpents
the dark waters hardly a memory

everything before was confusion
narrow
my thoughts outside
my soul constricted
and so was my bewilderment
I was two things at once
suffering and deserving of this suffering

I feel hands
they come to me in my dreams
their long fingers search for my heart
they stop and listen to its beat
they caress me
and create springs in stars

all is willing and sweet and slow
you widened *cor meum* in every beat
with this fountain the castle grows
emanating emanating

## QUINTO PELDAÑO
Tesoros y deleites

> Aspira a lo celeste,
> que siempre dura
> —TERESA DE ÁVILA

I

no queriendo ver
me muestra más
el sol desde su llama

en este peldaño
el viento nombra

los sentidos se adormecen
las potencias
las fuerzas del cuerpo
no sirven en el quinto peldaño

hijitas
no dilatemos la subida
buscando las razones
la dulce voz nos lleva
a la bodega del vino

esa bodega
donde está el néctar
es adentro
profundo
en el eje del alma

II

la dulce voz dice
hay que morir
en una muerte sabrosa
y gozar el nuevo día

## THE FIFTH STEP

Treasures and Delights

> Aim for the heavenly,
> which always endures
> —TERESA OF AVILA

I

not wanting to see
it shows me more
the sun from its flame

on this step
that the wind names

my senses go numb
my strength
my body's forces
don't work on the fifth step

oh my daughters
let's not prolong our ascent
searching for reasons
the tender voice leads us
to the wine cellar

that cellar
full of nectar
sits deep within
built upon
the soul's axis

II

the tender voice says
we must die
a pleasant death
and delight in the new day

## III

una mente sosegada
ilumina a las demás
el camino recorrido
ensancha el castillo
la verdadera unión
es descanso en el cuerpo
hermanas
hay que morir para vivir
esta es la victoria
la unión verdadera

## IV

quisiera decirles
pero entiendan
naufrago entre sonidos

## SESTO PELDAÑO
Heridas

> Mira que el amor es fuerte;
> vida no me seas molesta,
> mira que solo me resta,
> para ganarte perderte.
> —TERESA DE ÁVILA

## I

debo salir
procurar la soledad
apaguen la luz
que sean sus ojos
la lumbre del castillo

en el sesto peldaño
recios dolores preñan el cuerpo
la dulce voz dice paciencia

III

a quiet mind
illuminates others
the road traveled
stretches towards the castle
the truest union
is the body's rest
sisters
you must die in order to live
this is victory
the truest union

IV

I'd like to tell them
but they understand
I sink between sounds

## SIXTH STEP
Wounds

> See that love is strong;
> life, leave me be;
> to win You, to lose You—
> look at what's left of me.
> —TERESA OF AVILA

I

I must leave
in search of solitude
turn off the light
so your eyes may be
the castle's glow

on the sixth step
a heavy pain fills my body
the tender voice says *patience*

dice tallo de maíz
hijitas
estamos a la espera de las lluvias
y soñamos con el mar
ayer volvió a aparecer mientras dormía
construíamos castillos
luego venían olas blanquecinas
a llevárselo todo

quisiera decirles
pero las palabras me golpean los labios
quisiera obedecer el recado
pero escribo dando vueltas
con esta grita en el pecho
con esta lanza en la lengua

II

les digo quédense
hermanas
esperen el rayo
aunque no se escuche
hace un temblor en el alma
quema un poco
por lo mismo hiere tanto
dejando ganas de padecer más

III

hay otras maneras de despertar
no solo el sol alumbra
el aliento toca
brilla y dicta palabras
con poco se entiende harto
y queda un sosiego consoladísimo
por muy mucho tiempo

it says *stalk of maize*
oh my daughters
we're waiting for the rains
and we dream of the sea
it returned yesterday while I slept
we built castles
but later white waves came
and washed them all away

I'd like to tell you
but the words crash against my lips
I'd like to obey the message
but I write myself in circles
with this scream in my chest
with this spear on my tongue

II

oh sisters
I tell you to stay
and wait for the lightning bolt
though unheard
it shakes the soul
it burns a little
and wounds so much
but still you want to suffer more

III

there are other ways of awakening
besides the burning sun
breath touches
shines and dictates words
a little is enough to understand
and it remains a comforting calm
for a very long time

IV

el dulce susurro
su azulada voz saturada del veneno del mundo
muestra algunos secretos en este peldaño
manantiales resplandecientes en el desierto
inician nuevas andanzas originarias
pactos secretos en la cima de los adentros
destellos y fragmentos de espacio inexistente
nada    nada    nada
no les he dicho nada
y se llena el pecho de una grita
de una grita intoxicada que me condena


V

hijitas mías
no puedo resistirme al vuelo
ese vértigo etéreo de la voz
en mis paisajes más extraños

timbra el pulso en la roca del corazón
se oye el tiempo y su efecto exponencial
la voz gigante ahora poderosa
sostiene el océano
mi conciencia sopla
una velocidad temible me apresa
y este peldaño se vuelve marejada
suben las aguas
salen de cause
es así como el dulce susurro aparece
que no sé bien si es cosa de nombre


VI

desde la sombra viene la esfera azul
aparece proyectada hacia el vacío
atraviesa el cuerpo los cuerpos

IV

the tender voice
its blue whisper steeped in the world's poison
reveals a few secrets on this step
shining springs in the desert
begin new adventures at their origins
secret pacts on the highest peaks within me
flashes and fragments of nonexistent space
nothing    nothing    nothing
I've told them nothing
and a scream fills my chest
a toxic scream that damns me

V

oh my daughters
I cannot resist flight
the voice's eternal vertigo
in my most alien landscapes

the pulse rings in the rock of my heart
time and its exponential effect are heard
now the giant voice is powerful
it holds the ocean
my conscience blows
a fearful speed seizes me
and this step swells into a raging sea
the waters rise
they lose their course
and thus the tender whisper appears
I don't know if this is a named thing

VI

from the shadow a blue sphere arrives
as if projected across the void
it pierces the body the bodies

al inicio es un grano de arena
pronto se dilata manto circular
la respiración acompaña su ritmo
y vuelve a ser ínfima diminuto hálito
sigue este juego que no sabré explicar
ni por qué lo he venido a decir

## VII

siento las quiebras de la grita
son canciones repetidas
que decido no escuchar
el dulce susurro dice soy luz
hijitas
les digo
es barranco

## VIII

oigo cara a cara
la voz me mira
entra preguntando
esto puede tomar siglos
quiere    quiere
podría decir no
disfrazar el barranco
construir falsos puentes

## IX

susurra sea arcilla
digiera el veneno
no hable de las heridas
no hable
no hable
sea arcilla

at first it's a grain of sand
soon it expands into a circular mantle
my breathing accompanies its rhythm
and it again becomes my smallest breath
it continues this game that I won't know how to explain
or why I even tried to

VII

I sense that in my scream's brokenness
are repeated songs
that I choose not to listen to
the whisper says *I am light*
oh my daughters
I tell you this voice
is a ravine

VIII

I listen face-to-face
the voice looks at me
it comes in asking
this could take centuries
it wants     it wants
I could say no
disguise the ravine
build false bridges

IX

whisper
turn into clay
absorb the poison
do not speak of wounds
do not speak do not speak
turn into clay

## X

hijitas
se muestra
son diversas sus formas

## XI

los padecimientos del alma
esa lanza apuntando
el centro de lo incorpóreo
ese dolor sin carne
con qué palabras se explica

### SÉTIMO PELDAÑO
Encuentro

> No está la cosa en pensar mucho,
> sino en amar mucho,
> y así lo que más os despertare a amar,
> eso haced.
> —TERESA DE ÁVILA

## I

todo espera ser dicho
pero no sabemos cómo
solo intuimos
la belleza

## II

el esperado encuentro
la dulce voz derramada
la mente abierta
los colores no existen
ni el sonido
algo ocurre
un saber inesperado
una delicia sostenida

## X

my daughters
it shows
its diverse forms

## XI

the tribulations of the spirit
that brandished spear
the incorporeal center
that fleshless pain
what words can explain it?

## SEVENTH STEP
Encounter

> There is nothing in thinking deeply,
> if one does not love deeply,
> and so I will awaken you to love,
> so you will.
> —TERESA OF AVILA

## I

everything waits to be said
but we don't know how
we only sense
beauty

## II

the awaited encounter
the tender voice spilled
the mind open
the colors don't exist
nor the sound
something happens
unexpected knowledge
sustained joy

**III**

un olvido de sí
la soledad en compañía
el silencio
el sosiego

**IV**

este deleite
hermanas
este encandilarse sin mirar

III

a forgetting of the self
solitude among company
silence
tranquility

IV

this joy
oh sisters
this unseen light within

# Migración

Dejar la tierra es herida y cicatriz

Algunos salen con un raspón
de la primera caída desde la bicicleta
o las marcas de las primeras vacunas

Otros exhiben en sus dedos cortes de papel
presentan documentos migratorios
solicitudes de asilo o refugio

Hay manos que presentan picaduras y ampollas

Hay suturas bellas
bajo textiles caros
y ácido hialurónico

Hay queloides también
que crecen y deforman
por descuido, condición genética, mala praxis
un seguro impagable
o un hospital en ruinas

Pequeñas, grandes
cortas, largas
huellas de navajas
quemaduras y balas

Hay cicatrices hechas tatuajes
testimonios y relatos en tinta

Hay cicatrices bajo la piel
que afloran por fotografías
pesadillas, libros

## Migration

Leaving our land is wound and scar

Some go with scratches
from their first bike crashes
or pricks from their first vaccines

Others reveal the paper cuts on their fingers
when they present their documents
and ask for asylum or refuge

There are hands with stings and boils

There are beautiful sutures
beneath expensive fabric
and hyaluronic acid

There are keloids too
that grow deformed
by neglect, genetics, bad praxis
unpaid premiums
or a hospital in ruins

Tall, short
big and small
we wear the marks of knives,
burns, and bullets

There are tattooed-over scars
records and testimonies in ink

And the scars beneath the skin too
that resurface for photographs
nightmares, books

canciones, noticias
voces de videollamadas
voces grabadas y reproducidas una y otra vez desde el celular

Dejar la tierra es negación y resiliencia
desarraigo y nostalgia
Es instinto de supervivencia
sobre nuestro manto de retazos geopolíticos
raídos y vueltos a remendar

songs, the news
voices on WhatsApp calls
messages listened to again and again

Leaving this land is repudiation and resilience
rootlessness and longing
It's our instinct to survive
on this geopolitical patchwork quilt
worn threadbare but sewn up again

## Lazos

*a Carola*

La cuerda
llama a los cielos
suspende
enmudece

~

Ariadna, me guías hasta la belleza.
Por favor, sácame del laberinto.
Escucho a quienes me llaman.
Sus voces están en mi mente y en mi corazón.
Escucho el viento, escucho los pájaros.
Escucho la lluvia, huelo la tierra húmeda.

Veo sombras que opacan los colores.
Hay ruidos que distorsionan los violines.
El llanto me hace ver hilos colgantes.
Sácame de la caverna, por favor.

~

La respiración aúna la vida con el ser, Ariadna.

Inhalemos.

Como personajes de Chagall.
Como nubes de Calder.
Como el aire de Velázquez.

Elevémonos.

~

Los seres preciados despiertan el instinto de muerte. El amor se enraíza,
sus ramas abrazan los cuerpos. Teme por su abrupta desaparición.

## Bonds

*for Carola*

The rope
calls to the heavens
it hangs there
and silences

⁓

Ariadne, you guide me to beauty.
Please, lead me from this labyrinth.
I listen to those who call.
Their voices in my mind, in my heart.
I listen to the wind, I listen to the birds.
I listen to the rain, I smell the damp earth.

I see shadows. They darken all the colors.
They tangle the sound of violins.
With a cry I see the hanging threads.
Please, lead me from this cavern.

⁓

Breathing connects life and being, Ariadne.

Let us take a breath.

Like Chagall's figures.
Like Calder's clouds.
Like the air of Velázquez.

Let us rise.

⁓

Loved ones wake up at the moment of death. Love takes root, branches
embrace their bodies. Love fears for its sudden end.

La cuerda está rota, Ariadna.
Puedo ver las luciérnagas.

~

The rope is broken, Ariadne.
I can see the fireflies.

## Coraza

Un cuerpo áspero
opaco
se entrega a otro
displicente
da efímero placer
deja su olor
su acritud
y su piel muerta

Una máscara sonriente
oculta la pena
La ropa larga y angosta
encubre el descuido
los meses de abandono

Vergüenza

Un cuerpo cansado
hastiado
desnutrido
que cree en el deber
extraña el origen
y anhela la tierra
fundirse con la tierra

## Shell

A ragged and opaque
body submits
to someone else
complacently
gives ephemeral pleasure
leaves its scent
its bitterness
and its dead skin

A smiling mask
covers the pain
Long and tight clothes
conceal carelessness
months of neglect

Shame

A body
run down
and malnourished
believes in duty
misses its homeland
longs for the soil
sinks into the soil

## Remanentes

Huellas profundas en el cemento
que están, pero se ignoran

La sangre austral
rememora a la sangre de una "tierra de (des)gracia"

Instantes de caos y violencia
reviven fantasmas
de cráneos
pechos
rostros
baleados

El odio
con latencia fraticida
siembra temores de errancia
una nueva errancia

*¿Y qué haremos con tanta ceniza?*

El suelo irregular
vidrios rotos
rocas desfigurantes
son de la escena de guerra

Gases irritantes
cuerpos magullados
caen en el asfalto caliente

*¿Y qué haremos con tanta ceniza?*

## Remnants

Deep wounds in the concrete
There, but ignored

This southern blood
like the blood of the "Land of (dis)Grace"[1]

Moments of chaos and violence
revive ghosts
of shot-out
skulls
chests
faces

Hatred
with murderous deliberation
sows fear of wandering
a new wandering

*And what will we do with all this ash?*

Uneven ground
broken glass
disfiguring rocks
a scene of war

Poison gas
bruised bodies
fall to the hot asphalt

*And what will we do with all this ash?*

---

1. "The Land of Grace" was a nickname given by Christopher Columbus to the region that is now present-day Venezuela.

Euforia de unos
llanto de otros
por momentos se hacen invisibles

Las ilusiones se rompen
el caos es el rey
y la incertidumbre es la reina

*¿Y qué haremos con tanta ceniza?*

El fuego consume
los artificios foráneos
emergen del humo viejas pesadillas

El hollín llega hasta el fondo
oscurece la piel
opaca toda certeza posible

*¿Y qué haremos con tanta ceniza?*

Euphoria for some
tears for others
sometimes invisible

Illusions are broken
chaos is king
and uncertainty his queen

*And what will we do with all this ash?*

The fire consumes
foreign ruses
old nightmares emerge from the smoke

The soot falls within us
it smears our skin
blots out all certainty

*And what will we do with all this ash?*

T

A ti
ni agua
que engendraste exiliados del mundo
secaste el sustento
y la piel
que envuelve la comida descompuesta

Tú
reventaste el pecho
que eyecta sangre
que corre por años
se pudre
como tus entrañas

Tus padres
reflejos infames
te relataron sofismas
pesadillas
pestes
resentimiento
aturden por generaciones

Tus sirenas cantan tus mentiras
que se clavan en ojos y oídos
lobotomizan

Chispas ciegan
zumbidos atraviesan cabezas
rebeldes
por "accidente"
"enfrentamiento"
"suicidio"
Lo orquestan filas y uniformes
Detrás de ellos escupes odio
en tu trono de mierda

T

For you
not even water
You who begot the exiles of the world
You who dried up their livelihood
and the skin
that holds festered food

You
battered the torso
which spurts blood
that runs for years
It rots
like your entrails

Your forefathers
vile reflections who taught you
the empty rhetoric
nightmares
plagues
and resentment
that deafen generations

Your Sirens sing your lies
which bore through eyes and ears
like orbitoclasts

Sparks blind prisoners
A buzzing pierces the skulls
of rebels
by "accident"
"misbehavior"
or "suicide"
Uniforms and ranks orchestrate
but behind them you spit your hatred
from your throne of shit

Con alicate arrancas
la juventud
las raíces
la voz
el trabajo
las uñas
los dientes
los tendones
la cordura
el miedo a la muerte

Con electricidad enciendes
dolor
terror
desesperación
carne

Bailas sobre cadáveres
haces aquelarre de miseria
atropellas vulnerables con vehículos
frente a millones
de cómplices

Diriges circos judiciales
contra acusados torturados
te aplauden tus zalameros
frente a la podredumbre

Sueltas monstruos y demonios
devoradores de inocencia
bestias de fuego y plomo

Encarcelas y apaleas
en un domo
en cuartos de locos

With pliers you rip out
youth
roots
voices
work
fingernails
teeth
tendons
sanity
the fear of death

With electricity you light up
pain
terror
desperation
flesh

You dance over bodies
you host a coven of misery
you run down the vulnerable with vehicles
in front of millions
of accomplices

You oversee judicial circuses
against tortured defendants
The bootlickers still applaud you
though they know of your corruption

You set loose monsters and demons
beasts of fire and lead
that feed on innocence

You jail and beat prisoners
in the Dome[1]
in the madhouses

---

1. The Helicoide, a prison and torture facility in Caracas.

en una sepultura gélida
siempre blanca

Saqueas la tierra noble
envenenas los ríos
matas a sus criaturas
con tu codicia

Eructas moscas
que se posan sobre tus aduladores
Repartes botines
Compras silencio
Crías burócratas
Les lanzas cebo a los farsantes
roen desperdicios
a tus pies

Estrangulas las luces
las corrientes
los motores
las almas hambrientas
los enfermos

Persigues las palabras
que punzan tus miedos
las callas
las desapareces

Innombrable maldito
húndete con tu séquito
y tu andamio
en tus mazmorras
en las sombras
en la nada

in a tomb[2]
always kept frigid and white

You loot the noble land
you poison the rivers
you kill their creatures
with your greed

You belch up flies
that land on your flatterers
You hand them plunder
You buy silence
You raise bureaucrats
You throw slop to the frauds
who gnaw the scraps
at your feet

You choke out the lights
the electricity
the motors
the hungry
the sick

You persecute the words
that fill your fears
Silenced
disappeared

Unspeakable Pig
May you sink with your cronies
and your courtiers
into your dungeons
into the shadows
into nothingness

---

2. The Tomb, an underground torture facility located beneath the Bolivarian Intelligence Service (SEBIN) headquarters in Caracas. The facility specializes in "white torture," that is, extended sensory deprivation. The facility is a brief walk from the poet's childhood home.

# Escombros

La brisa y la sal resguardan tumbas de barro.
Bloques y zinc
arropan familias mordidas por la lluvia.
Ellos no pudieron oponerse a la Naturaleza
ni a las nuevas leyes
ni a las promesas finiseculares
que se aglomeraban y petrificaban
frente al mar.

De aquellos niños se borran los rostros y los nombres.

⌣

Abandonados quedan los campos.
Los arbustos crecen sobre la tierra baldía
y los expoliados.

Los edificios derruidos hieden a humedad.
Cuerpos se camuflan
con la basura y la chatarra.

⌣

Rómulo, los brujos profanaron tus huesos.
Ya nadie lee *Doña Bárbara*.

⌣

El aire tiembla.
El viento arrastra las hojas
negras
de los libros quemados.

El jardín cromático se seca.

# Ruins

*December 1999, the Vargas tragedy*

The breeze and salt guard muddy graves.
Cinder blocks and zinc
blanket families bitten by rain.
They couldn't fight against nature
or the new laws
or the turn-of-the-century promises
that jam them together
petrified in front of the sea.

The names and faces of those children, erased.

⁓

The fields are abandoned.
Bushes grow across the looted land
and the corpses of those who lived there.

The leaning houses reek of rot.
Bodies hide beneath
garbage and sheet metal.

⁓

Rómulo Gallegos, the thieves desecrated your bones in a ritual
and still nobody will read *Doña Bárbara*.

⁓

The air trembles.
The black pages
of burned books blow
with the wind.

The university gardens dry out.

De esa casa solo hay sombra.

—

Los niños del nuevo siglo se acuestan.
Sus barriguitas apenas resisten el último bocado del día.
Sueñan con algo más que escombros.
Cierran los ojos
arrullados por la lluvia.

The house couldn't defeat the shadows.

⁓

The children of the new century are put to bed
their stomachs still hungry after the day's scraps.
They dream of something more than ruins
their eyes closed
lulled to sleep by the rain.

## Los topos

Suelo ir a pie por el boulevard o por la Casanova para llegar hasta Zona Rental. El recorrido toma alrededor de treinta y cinco minutos. Bajo tierra los topos se desplazan en una fracción de ese tiempo, si es que la desidia no detiene los trenes. Un descarrilamiento, falla eléctrica o arrollamiento destruye toda expectativa temporal; más bien acaba con cualquier expectativa. La incertidumbre es el único principio.

Cada vez que descendemos por las escaleras, nos convierten en topos. La desidia alarga el reencuentro con el exterior. Desarrolla la adaptación a la penumbra, el calor estancado, el olor a humedad, la aspereza de los túneles, el sonido de las goteras y de las piezas rompiéndose.

Nos ciegan ante las ideas convencionales de normalidad y civilidad, ya que empujar, insultar, correr por los andenes, gritar e ignorar cualquier consideración por el otro es la anomia subterránea.

"Coño de la madre," gruñe un topo cuando otro dejó caer su desesperación sobre los rieles.

Cercana y más profunda que los andenes existe una red de túneles de varios estratos. Sobre ella se han publicado artículos de prensa e informes. Allí algunos topos fueron retenidos completamente. No permanecen en la penumbra, sino en la luz fluorescente. Sienten mucho frío en vez de calor. Ven muros blancos en lugar de baldosas y láminas multicolores.

Regreso a casa tras buscar medicinas para mi abuela. En el camino veo artistas callejeros, tiendas medio vacías e individuos deambulando. Pienso en que a veces, cuando voy en tren, olvido que me convierten en un topo y que algunos de ellos saben más sobre la incertidumbre y la desidia, pues hace mucho que no se suben a un tren.

# Moles

*La Tumba (The Tomb) is an underground detention facility of a tower in Caracas, Venezuela, that serves as the headquarters for the Bolivarian Intelligence Service (SEBIN). It was initially designed as offices for the Caracas Metro.*

I usually walk down the boulevard or the Casanova to get to the Zona Rental projects. This takes about thirty-five minutes. The moles move underground in a fraction of the time, that is, if the trains aren't stopped by neglect. A derailment, an electrical failure, or a hit-and-run shreds any schedule, kills any expectation of punctuality. Uncertainty: our only guiding principle.

Whenever we descend those stairs, they turn us into moles. Their negligence drags out the time until we can see the world above ground again. We become accustomed to the gloom, the sluggish heat, the damp smell, the harshness of those tunnels, the sounds of dripping water, of pieces breaking loose.

They've made us blind to normalcy, to civility. Pushing and cursing, running for the platforms, screaming and ignoring anyone else: our subterranean anomie.

One mole growls *motherfucker* when another drops his despair to the rails.

Near the platforms, but deeper still, there is a different network of tunnels. Organizations have published reports on it. Some moles are held there permanently. Not in shadow but in fluorescent light. They feel the cold instead of heat, stare at white walls instead of multicolored tiles.

I walk home after searching for medicine for my grandmother. On the way, I see homeless artists, half-empty shops, all the people wandering about. I think of how, when I travel by train, I forget that they've turned me into a mole too—they who are well versed in uncertainty and neglect, who haven't had to take the train in years.

## Sueño verde

Veo tus manos en la penumbra
y en las hojas
acariciadas por el viento

toman los hibiscus
para la amada
que llora frente al mar

Las manos escriben palabras
Palabras de risa
de fuego
de agua
de anhelo

Palabras tejidas de luces y brisa
caribeña
Palabras para la amada
triste

Las manos tocan el aire
siluetas ilusorias
el rostro lejano
los recuerdos arrancados
por la peste

Mis ojos buscan las manos
buscan sus bifurcaciones
la piel erizada
el instante del consuelo
el tiempo detenido

## Dream in Green

I see your hands in the half-light
and on leaves
caressed by wind

they pick the hibiscus
for their beloved
who weeps by the sea

Your hands write words
Words of laughter
of fire
of water
of desire

Words woven of light
and Caribbean breeze
Words for
a sad love

Your hands touch the air
quick silhouettes
your face far off
memories ripped away
by plague

My eyes search for your hands
they look for their creases
their raised hairs
a moment of comfort
time stopped

## Memorias

Orquídeas y copihues
las posé en mi pecho
y en mi vientre
secas están adheridas en versos
partituras
*bildungsromane*
conmigo estarán
hasta la última exhalación
o el próximo destierro

## Memories

Dry orchids and copihues
I arrange them on my chest
and womb
they are joined with verses
sheet music
bildungsromans
they'll be with me
until my final breath
or until I am exiled next

# Río

río hoy
río para dejarlo hasta mañana
río Amazonas
río Nilo
río por la geografía
río de sirenas lejanas
río por la cera en los oídos
río de gente
río de caras de raja
río, payaso
río de letanías
río de mantras
río de oraciones
río como loca
río de pastillas de fluoxetina
río de alegría
río de lágrimas
río de lugares comunes
río del menos común de los sentidos
río de mocos en el pañuelo
río de animales atropellados
río con doble acento
rio
río en presente del indicativo
río, si rieras . . .
reí, rey
ría
ríe, Heráclito
ríete, chico
río de música, mi sol
río de tranvías, altazores y aullidos
río con palabras
río de poesía
río (in)transitivo

## Laughter as River

my laughter flows today
my laughter flows, leaving everything until tomorrow
my laughter flows like the Amazon
my laughter flows like the Nile
my laughter flows across our geography
my laughter flows from the distant Sirens
my laughter flows through the wax we stuffed into our ears
my laughter flows through my people
my laughter shamelessly flows
my laughter flows, you clowns
my laughter flows with litanies
my laughter flows with mantras
my laughter flows with prayers
my laughter crazily flows
my laughter flows with fluoxetine pills
my laughter flows with happiness
my laughter flows with tears
my laughter flows with platitudes
my laughter flows with the most uncommon of sense
my laughter flows with snot in a handkerchief
my laughter flows with roadkill
my laughter flows through two languages
my laughter flowed
my laughter flows again in the present tense
my laughter flows if yours does
let your laughter flow, darling
let it flow
let your laughter flow, Heraclitus
let it flow, man
let your laughter flow with music, my love
my laughter flows with streetcars, parachutes, and howls
my laughter flows with words
my laughter flows with poetry
my laughter flows (in)transitively

río con los dientes rotos
río de barro
río de besos
río hasta el orgasmo
río de remolinos
río por la montaña
río de ojos de avellana
río hasta para por con sin de
río de Caronte
río de memoria
río porque sí
ríoríoríorío
¡ríooooo, carajo!
Río y lloro
Río y vivo
Río y sangre
Río, amor
río de golpe
río hasta la muerte
río hasta la desembocadura

my laughter flows with broken teeth
my laughter flows with mud
my laughter flows with kisses
my laughter flows and swirls
my laughter flows until orgasm
my laughter flows through the mountain
my laughter flows with hazel eyes
my laughter flows until for by of with without
my laughter flows with Charon
my laughter flows with memory
my laughter flows just for the hell of it
my laughter flowsflowsflowsflows
my laughter flooooows goddammit!
my laughter flows and I cry
my laughter flows and I live
my laughter flows with water and blood
my laughter flows with yours, my love
my laughter suddenly flows
my laughter flows until death
my laughter flows until the mouth of the river

## [En mi familia siempre hubo guerras]

En mi familia siempre hubo guerras
      Silenciosas
              Largas
Al terminarse todos se alegraban
Ya era tarde      para mí
Apilado en un montón de cadáveres

## [In my family we always fought]

In my family we always fought
    A long
           And silent war
When it ended everyone was happy
But it was too late      for me
Piled upon a mountain of corpses

## [Seguí una hilera de hormigas]

Seguí una hilera de hormigas que me llevaron hasta el bosque Aokigahara.
Al principio quería ir sobre la espalda de mi madre,
A la que robé el puñado de cruces
Para protegerme del asedio de las brujas.
Caminé
Siguiendo los pasos de mis pasos,
Me transformé en árbol y me aplaudieron
Me talaron para que no se esparciera mi memoria
Ni nunca nadie volviera a ver mis rasgos o mis gestos.
Mis manos son raíces que con torpeza resquebrajaron la tierra.
Mis manos con torpeza reclaman la soga.
A mi madre le pedí mi herencia, se acercó a mi oído
Y susurró *la sumisión es un arma*.
Me dio la espalda y antes de morir me bendijo con veneno.
Este bosque es mi herida, un sangrado de epitafios.
Ahora me preguntas quién se ha llevado nuestra casa.
Tengo la misma edad que tú, mamá.
Venimos de una estirpe que se niega a salir del ritual de la sequía.
Y que tiene la palabra divorcio
En la punta de la lengua.

## [I followed a line of ants]


I followed a line of ants that led me to Aokigahara forest.
At first, I wanted to ride on the back of my mother
from whom I stole a fistful of crosses
to protect myself from the witches' siege.
I walked
following the steps of my steps.
I turned into a tree and they applauded me.
They cut me down so that my memory wouldn't be sowed.
Nobody returned to see my features or my gestures.
My hands are roots that clumsily cracked the earth.
My hands clumsily reclaim the rope.
I asked my mother for my heritage, she drew close and into my ear
whispered *submission is a weapon.*
She turned her back to me and before dying blessed me with venom.
This forest is my wound, a bleeding of epitaphs.
Now you ask me, "Who has stolen our house?"
We're the same age, Mom.
We come from a lineage that refuses to leave behind the ritual of drought.
That has the word *divorce*
on the tip of its tongue.

# [Tengo dos semillas que me dio mi padre]

Tengo dos semillas que me dio mi padre
Las guardo debajo de mis párpados
Van en sentido retrógrado, hasta volverse una célula imprecisa
He sido obligado a respirar despacio, a torcerle
El decimotercer lazo a la muerte
Mi soledad es un mundo de pájaros
Tengo la tercera costilla rota
La atmósfera me aplasta
La delgadez me acuna
La inmortalidad no se ha llevado mi memoria
Mi raza está diluida en pena
El hilo de mi descendencia me sigue desde lejos
Nací en aquelarre
Leche negra me fortificó
No hago más que gritar augurios
No puedo caminar erguido, no puedo
Mi hermana fue concebida en luna menguante
Mientras a mí me criaban los lobos
Mi sendero no es claro, está tibio
Y la sumisión me congela . . .

## [My father gave me two seeds]

My father gave me two seeds
I keep them under my eyelids
They retrograde until they become amorphous cells
I've been forced to breathe slowly, to twist
death's thirteenth knot
My solitude is a world of birds
My third rib is broken
The atmosphere crushes me
Gauntness cradles me
Immortality hasn't stolen my memory
My race is diluted with grief
The thread of my lineage follows me from afar
I was born in a coven
Black milk nourished me
I can only shout omens
I can't walk upright, I can't
My sister was conceived in a waning moon
while I was raised by wolves
My path isn't clear, it's tepid
And submission freezes me . . .

## [Llevas piedras porosas en tu estómago]

Llevas piedras porosas en tu estómago y eres la hija de Olokun, mi hermana. Te acordarás de los días de persignaciones antes del desayuno, el almuerzo y la cena. Casi ciego puse en claro mi náusea, que nadie te vea el pliegue. La flatulencia saca de adentro secuelas colgantes. Hermana, los dientes no nos sobran, son las 8 p.m. y no ha muerto la mosca; ronda en los siete platos de sopa. Te serví mi carroña pulida y añejada porque de nuestra madre sólo escuchamos sus tripas. Ella no tiene la culpa pero fue la primera en servirnos una mesa de patas anchas, sal y aire, espantando las ansias hasta el otro día. Permíteme, por favor, restaurar mi fuerza para golpearte, hermana, justo en la boca. Que el golpe desuelle tu estómago, para que de una vez por todas se te quite el hambre.

## [You carry porous stones in your stomach]


You carry porous stones in your stomach. You are the daughter of Olokun, my sister. You'll remember the days of the sign of the cross before breakfast, lunch, and dinner. Nearly blind, I make my nausea clear, may no one see your skin's hungry folds. The flatulence escapes from hanging sequelae. Sister, we don't have any teeth left, it's 8:00 p.m. and the fly hasn't died; it prowls above seven soup plates. I served you my polished and aged carrion because we only hear our mother's gut. It's not her fault, but she was the first to serve us an empty table, salt, and air, scaring off the aches until another day. Please, let me regain my strength so I might hit you, sister, right in the mouth. May the blow fly your stomach and ease your hunger once and for all.

## [Alimentaste al cachorro con tu teta blanca]

Alimentaste al cachorro con tu teta blanca, con tu espesa leche azulada parecida a la de nuestra madre. No lograste conciliar el sueño después de un día largo, soñaste apenas con el cachorro. ¿De dónde comenzó a enmudecer tu saliva? ¿Dónde comenzaste a divagar en la pesadilla? Ahora ya lo sabes: te fue negado, exiliada de tu propio sueño. No podrás imaginarte una existencia respetable e imaginar tu vida despierta para siempre. Despertarás con sabor a insecto, de esos que devoraste durante la pesadilla, amargos y jugosos. Tendrás el recuerdo de su textura en tu lengua. El cachorro ha existido en tu memoria, ha gozado en tu niñez, ha crecido hasta transformarse en un inmenso lobo de afilados dientes, para venir a morder el palpitante órgano del sueño.

## [You nourished the cub on your white teat]

You nourished the cub on your white teat with your thick blue milk, like that of our mother. You couldn't fall asleep after a long day, you hardly dreamed of the cub. Where did your saliva begin to grow mute? Where did you begin to stray in your nightmare? Now you know: it was denied from you, exiled from your own dream. You won't be able to imagine a decent existence for yourself, you imagine your life awake forever. You'll wake up with the taste of insects in your mouth, those you devoured in your nightmare, bitter and rare. You'll remember their texture across your tongue. The cub has lived in your memory, taken pleasure in your girlhood, grown into an enormous wolf with sharp teeth, come to bite the palpitating organ of your dream.

## [En el mismo espejo donde dejé mi máscara y mis dedos]

En el mismo espejo donde dejé mi máscara y mis dedos
Mi abuela la clarividente asustada sabía que
Iba a repetir hábitos en cualquier circunstancia
Que me quedaría esperándola en su resurrección
De alas frías
En un momento en que los perros ladraban
Demasiado y yo negaba mis oídos a la premonición
Estaba claro
Me saldría espuma por la boca
Me rozarías con agua bendita
Vomitarías ataduras
Consultarías al decálogo de Aries tocándome
La frente
Tenía fiebre, abuela
Debí saberlo, que al llegar al mismo suelo
Que el tuyo me temblaría todo
La premonición seguía su curso
Santifícame para siempre
Sobre una mortaja verde
Santifícame para siempre
Con un plato lleno de moscas
Tiento tu última letanía.

## [In the same mirror where I left my mask and fingers]

In the same mirror where I left my mask and fingers
My grandmother, the frightened clairvoyant, learned that
She'd fall into the same habits no matter what
That I'd be left waiting for her at her cold-winged
Resurrection
In a moment when the dogs barked too much
And I surrendered my ears to the premonition
It was clear
My mouth would foam
You'd graze me with holy water
You'd vomit tethers
You'd read the Decalogue of Aries while touching
My forehead
I had a fever, Grandmother
I should've known that I'd tremble like this,
Arriving to the same soil as you
The premonition continued its course
Sanctify me forever
On a green shroud
Sanctify me forever
With a dish full of flies
I tempt your final litany.

GERARDO ARÍSTIDES RIVODÓ

# tantra

*a mi tía*

si supieras
que ahora emprendo
nuevo viaje
un trazo limpio
en lo secreto
si supieras
esta tierra pura
para decirnos
luz ilimitada
joya
en el silencio
si supieras que construyo
un país
de nadie conocido
para que tú seas
junto a todo
en un abrazo

tantra

*for my aunt*

if you knew
that I now embark
on a new journey
a clean pen stroke
in secret
if you knew
of this pure earth
to tell us
limitless light
jewel
in the silence
if you knew I'm building
a country
of nobody known
so you may be
together with everything
in an embrace

## [no la palabra sino el silencio]


no la palabra sino el silencio
ese paisaje coronado de tristezas
el despeño del pájaro
que mora mustio
                tras la niebla
el sesgo
lo más colmado
su sombra
su sombra
no digas más
no hay más
cerca están todos los verdugos
que juzgan la que eres
y el espíritu celeste que no asiste
a lo desesperado
a lo difícil que te habita
y tiemblas
¿de qué reino sin luz el designio
que consagró esta imagen
tambaleante -corroída
a la ausencia de sí misma?
reza las ruinas
de una pupila ciega
abierta al horizonte
reza el horror
lo que te extirpa
lo que te hunde
en el crepúsculo de ti misma
esa frontera para nadie que te hace
el mar
la piedra
la desolación
                    reza tus rostros
que devienen en incesantes fugas

## [not the word but the silence]


not the word but the silence
that landscape crowned in sorrow
the plummet of the bird
who dwells withered
                              beyond the fog
askew
saturated
its shadow
its shadow
say no more
there is no more
every executioner draws near
to judge who you are
as does the celestial spirit who doesn't lift
the hopelessness
the difficulty that inhabits you
and you tremble
and ask from which lightless kingdom
came the design that consecrated
this faltering image, corroded
in the absence of the self?
pray to the ruins
of a blind pupil
that opened to the horizon
pray to the horror
that extracts you
that sinks you
into the twilight of yourself
that border for nobody that makes you
the sea
the stone
desolation
                    pray to your faces
that become ceaseless

sin hogar
reza los poros
el cuerpo
rézate a ti    desgarrada
donde quebrantas el silencio
y haces el poema
reza el pájaro
empozado
en el estanque

and wandering fugues
pray to the pores
to the body
pray to yourself    torn
where you break the silence
and make the poem
pray to the bird
that sank
into the pond

## todo borrado

me acostumbraré al presagio
de una casa vacía
al vuelo que dibujas
sobre cielos penitentes
a la rotura de un pájaro
en paisajes desolados
vistos      detrás de las ventanas
a ese signo irrevocable de flor
trunca de lluvia entre tus manos
al espesor de niebla
donde melodías de nieves
invocan solo
un lánguido silencio
labio por labio
agua por agua
gris/
        todo borrado

## everything erased

I'll get used to the omen
of an empty house
to the flight that you draw
on penitent skies
to the brokenness of a bird
in a barren landscape
seen      from behind the windows
to that irrevocable flower sign
ruined by rain between your hands
to the depth of fog
where the melodies of frost
invoke only
a languid silence
lip for lip
water for water
gray/
          everything erased

## [para mi cuerpo]

para mi cuerpo
el exilio
una partitura de nieve
la carencia
los adioses
la tormenta solitaria
lo muy oscuro
lo oscuro

para mis manos
la ofrenda
una oración ausente
y todo aquello
que no canta
la infancia
los miedos

el nunca en la palabra

[for my body]

for my body
exile
a score of snow
want
goodbyes
a lonely storm
the darkness
the dark

for my hands
an offering
an absent prayer
and everything
that doesn't sing
childhood
fear

the never within the word

[ser]


ser
solo ausencia
un movimiento en blanco
una nota suelta sobre el aire
hasta r o m p e r s e

ser
eco de lo que se fue
tan lejos        una voz

ser
al fondo
una palabra imposible
donde poder vivirse
donde poder nombrarse

[to be]


to be
only absence
a movement in white
a note loosed to the air
until b r e a k i n g

to be
an echo of what's gone
so far away        a voice

to be
at the end
an impossible word
where you can live
where you can be named

# [qué imposibilidad]

También la eternidad está llena de ojos.

—PAUL CELAN

qué imposibilidad
nos entregó a esta distancia?

qué signo oculto evaporó
el incendio de los labios?

lejos su sombra
su infinito cielo

el mordaz aullido de su cuerpo

la región dispuesta a salmo y cópula
deletreando el pulso de su arena

lejos ya el sueño
que precise el sacramento de su noche

el transparente bogar bajo su piel
los delirios lentos
el peligroso tremar
el afuera del tiempo

# [what impossibility]

Eternity too is full of eyes.

—PAUL CELAN

what impossibility
brought us this far?

what dark sign evaporated
the fire from your lips?

your far-flung shadow
your infinite sky

your body's biting howl

a region prepared for sex and psalm
spelling out your sand's pulse

now the dream recedes
demanding your night's sacrament

the diaphanous rowing beneath your skin
a slow madness
a dangerous shudder
the outside of time

## [esta mujer no es de sol]

esta mujer no es de sol
entre mis manos
en su rumor
invade lo oscuro
planta frases
en el nunca

se exilia
nadie sabe de sus nombres

esta mujer que soy
y que no soy
se automedica
para calmar
la casa con los hijos
siempre ausentes

traza horizontes
para ahuyentar la soledad
habla de pájaros
bajo las sábanas
me mira desde los espejos
calcula el frío
y entra en lo más íntimo

esta mujer no es de sol
entre mis manos
es el inevitable oficio de la lluvia
el perfume de una ciudad desconocida

## [this woman is not of the sun]

this woman is not of the sun
between my hands
within their murmur
the dark invades
it plants phrases
in the never

exiled
nobody knows her name

this woman that I am
and that I am not
self-medicates
to quiet
the house with children
always missing

she traces horizons
to stave off loneliness
she speaks of birds
beneath the sheets
she looks at me from every mirror
measures the cold
sinks into her deepest reaches

this woman is not of the sun
between my hands
the rain's inevitable office
a strange city's perfume

FERGIE CONTRERAS SALMEN

## 195

el mismo concreto
latente dolor
aferra al borde del risco

edificios por caer
los sonidos
de la tierra

enfermaron

por temblor
o dictadura

195

the same concrete
dormant pain
clings to the chasm's edge

the buildings on the verge of collapse
the earth's
sounds

sickened

by earthquake
or dictatorship

**182**

los suelos están muertos
son hormigas calcadas
polvo contraído

*calambres*

un pie que se detiene

arqueó otra vez
*el sodio*
se dobla
sangre aglutina

ahoga

la imposibilidad de matar

el goce

## 182

the land is dead
only crushed ants
infected dust

*cramps*

the foot stops

it arches once more
*the sodium*
it doubles
blood congeals

and drowns

impossible to kill

the jouissance

**235**

la carne instala arrebatos
impulsos
tonalidades dispares

marrón
violeta
un círculo de pequeños coágulos

*te ha gustado pintar desde siempre*

*acabas de percibirlo*

## 235

rage originates in the flesh
impulses
contrasting shades

brown
violet
a circle of little blood clots

*you've always liked to paint*

                              *but you just now realized*

# 307

recuerdas la clase de química

tu única norma universal
más allá de los arraigos
un apego
ambivalente

la materia

nada
crea
no
destruye

*se transforma*

307

you remember chemistry class

your only universal law
beyond the roots
an ambivalent
attachment

matter

nothing
created
nor
destroyed

*just transforms*

## 308

si lo malo
no es
evaporarse abre una forma
de ser

                                                   a escondidas

## 308

if trouble
isn't so
evaporating secretly
opens a way

                                        of being

## 198

por debajo cenizas
*y calma*

la autonomía busca
soledad
pide sanciones

al trino de las aves
la noche en su emigrar

los recuerdos se disipan

(no hay más luces)

quedan huérfanos
en vela

beneath the ashes
*and calm*

autonomy searches
for solitude
and demands sanctions

upon the birds' trilling
and night's migrating

the memories dissipate

(no more light)

orphans remain
in vigil

**219**

oídos inmutables
asilan ondas transparentes

partículas de oxígeno
inducen
sin tocar
inhalar involuntario

lo vital yace en el aire
respirar es inconsciente

219

immutable ears
grant asylum to invisible waves

particles of oxygen
induce
involuntary inhalations
undisturbed

vitality rests in the air
breathing is unconscious

## 220

tolerar la propia voz
en medio del océano

el eco de las olas
no absuelve

tras pactar con el lenguaje
la soledad presiona al habla

*el hilo está en el cuello*

puedes ahogar
o escucharte

## 220

bearing your own voice
in the middle of the ocean

the waves' echoes
aren't acquitted

after making a pact with language
solitude presses down upon speech

*the thread is in your neck*

you can drown
or listen to yourself

## Saudade I o El Viaje

¿Cómo se llama
Ese viaje que
Hace la mente
Ante la Cámara?

Tengo que describir
Las notas de
Un Nina Ricci
Mientras voy bajando
Las escaleras de
La plaza Altamira.

En medio de
una llamada médica,
Mi voz enumera
Síntomas de Covid,
Pero mis ojos
Ven el Ocaso
De Sabana Grande.

Mis dedos pulen
Con un paño
La plata mientras
Veo pinos y
La Colonia Tovar.

Tengo que levantar
La vista para
Ver el calendario,
No para concentrarme,
Sino para que
No se nuble
Mi vista cansada
Con la nostalgia.

## Saudade I or The Journey


What do you call
This journey made
By the mind before
The camera?

I have to describe
The notes of
A Nina Ricci perfume
While walking down
The stairs at
Plaza Altamira.

In the middle
Of a medical call,
My voice lists
COVID symptoms,
But my eyes
Watch the sunset
At Sabana Grande.

With a cloth
My fingers shine
Silver while
I watch the pines
Of Colonia Tovar.

I have to draw
My eyes to the calendar.
Not to concentrate,
But so that
My tired gaze
Doesn't cloud
With longing.

## Saudade II o Migrar

Migrar también es saber leer mapas, saber de mapas.
Es aprender a distinguir los cambios entre líneas de metro,
saber qué hora es demasiado temprano, o demasiado tarde,
confirmar las sospechas de cuando alguien miente, o no le importas.

Migrar también es olvidar los arreboles de las cinco de la tarde
por los atardeceres ígneos de un día gris de invierno,
el olor del cuarto de costura por el de la estufa en medio de la sala,
las luces del comedor a medianoche por la de tu nueva lámpara.

Migrar también es decir para tus adentros que el ticket
que compraste para ese concierto compensa todos esos
a los que no fuiste ni irás, y no duele tanto el no tomar
la mano de tus amigos ausentes cuando suena Jubilee Street.

Migrar también es no saber qué hacer con los hados
que te ayudaron a sobrellevar la miseria en tu primera casa.
No poder cambiarlos, ni matarlos, ni dejarlos bajo el hielo,
no poder ignorarlos con tu ropa nueva, o las frutas de la estación.

Quizás dejarlos dormir, por ahora, en esa gaveta dentro de tu corazón,
hasta que aprendan tu nueva lengua, hasta que puedas compartirlos
con alguien que no quiera pisarlos, o se aburra de ellos o de ti,
y vuelvas a verle el sentido a la magia y al amarillo del mundo.

## Saudade II or Migration

Migration also means knowing how to read maps, to know about maps.
It's learning to navigate the changes between metro lines,
knowing what time is too early or too late,
confirming your suspicions when someone lies, when you don't matter to them.

Migration also means forgetting the clouds that would glow red
at five in the afternoon in the igneous sunset of a gray winter's day,
the smell of the woodstove in the middle of the sewing room,
the dining room's soft light at midnight beneath your new lamp.

Migration also means telling yourself that the ticket
you bought for that concert makes up for all of those
that you never went to, the ones you'll never go to, that it doesn't hurt so much
to not hold the hand of your absent friends when "Jubilee Street" plays.

Migration also means not knowing what to do with the spirits
who helped you bear the misery of your first home,
unable to change them, or kill them, or leave them beneath the ice,
or ignore them with your new clothes or this season's fruit.

Maybe let them sleep, for now, in that drawer inside your heart
until they learn your new language, until they can be shared with someone
who doesn't want to step on them, who won't grow tired of them or you,
until once again you see the meaning of the magic and the yellow of the world.

## Por dentro, la noche avanza

De niña, leí un cuento sobre un señor al que no le gustaba la noche.
De niña, me quedaba hasta tarde mirando el faro de la televisión,
siguiendo al canto de sirena de las comiquitas y, años más tarde,
The Film Zone a la medianoche, hasta que el sueño me invadía,
entonces apagaba la tele y me acostaba a dormir.

De grande, llegué a volverme como aquel señor
que tras años de oscuridad, subió a la montaña
y paró el avance de la noche con un grito
para decirle lo infeliz que hacía a todo el pueblo.

Pero, como en el cuento, la noche avanza igual,
cubre los cielos, los cuartos vacíos, los proyectos
a medias y en blanco, el cansancio, las peleas y los
desahogos que nunca pasan del nudo en la garganta.

De grande, la noche espera a que la nube tormentosa
en mi pecho amaine, a que el cansancio y los deberes
de mañana me sobrepasen. A que, como el señor
del cuento, baje de mi montaña y me acueste a dormir.

Pero, como el señor del cuento, tampoco puedo dormir.
La noche en mí no habla, pero repite, hace eco que llena mi sueño,
y termino soñando con las estrellas que le formaré al día
siguiente una palabra, un movimiento, una tecla a la vez.

## Within Me, the Night Advances

When I was a girl, I read a story about a man who didn't like the night.
When I was a girl, I would stay up late watching the TV's beacon,
following the siren song of the cartoons and, years later,
the Film Zone at midnight, until drowsiness would invade me
and I'd turn off the screen and lay down to sleep.

As an adult, I started to become like that man
who, after years of darkness, climbed the mountain
to stop the night's advance with a cry,
declaring how unhappy it had made the entire town.

But, like in the story, the night came on anyway,
covered the skies, the empty rooms, the projects
half-done and blank, the weariness, the fights
and outpourings that would never rise from knotted throats.

As an adult, the night waits for the storm cloud
in my chest to die down, for weariness and tomorrow's
duties to overtake me, so that, like the man
in the story, I descend the mountain and lie down to sleep.

But, like that man, I can't rest either. The night within me
doesn't speak, it only repeats itself, an echo that fills my sleep,
and I end up dreaming of the stars I'll shape into the dark the next day,
following a word, a movement, one keystroke at a time.

ELIZARIA FLORES

# Río

El río de mi infancia arrastra piedras y neveras, mesas rotas, paraguas inservibles y anónimos cadáveres. En este río hay lágrimas y sangre, promesas incumplidas, suciedad y excremento y largas maldiciones junto a los restos de una casa y una diminuta mano de muñeca.

El río de mi infancia es una rabia inútil atravesando la ciudad, su miedo bordeando las esquinas, su amenaza. Pocas flores conocen sus orillas, los blanquísimos lirios, las minúsculas espigas venenosas.

El Guaire ha visto demasiado. La ciudad está desnuda y corre y baila y se emborracha. Celebra bodas de diamante o se pierde en despecho entre mercados y teléfonos.

La ciudad ayuna o se atiborra, se disfraza, ruega y blasfema y se resigna. Desnuda va asesinando en serie o suicidándose. Traiciona y apuñala.

A sus orillas, la maltratada exhibe sus heridas.
El río de mi infancia es un silencio atroz y un rencor minuciosamente entretejido.

## River

The river of my childhood drags along stones and refrigerators, broken tables, useless umbrellas, and anonymous corpses. In this river there are tears and blood, unfulfilled promises, muck and excrement, long-standing curses among the ruins of a house, and a doll's tiny hand.

The river of my childhood is a useless rage that pierces the city, its fear lining the street corners, lining their danger. Few flowers know the river's shores: the whitest lilies, small and venomous thorns.

The Guaire River has seen too much. The city is naked. It runs and it dances and it gets drunk. It celebrates diamond anniversaries or becomes lost in its spite between markets and telephones.

The city either fasts or fattens, it creates disguises, it roars and curses and it resigns itself. Naked, it embarks on a killing spree or kills itself. It's a traitor, a backstabber.

On its shores, the battered show their wounds.
The river of my childhood is atrocious silence, tightly woven resentment.

# Ciudad

Malquerida ciudad
Plaza asolada
Ciudad abandonada

De revuelta y saqueo
De plaga de insectos
De lluvia feroz y despiadada
De habitante indigno
Te levantas

Ciudad de huyentes
Ciudad de penitentes

Malquerida ciudad
Ciudad incendiada
Aniquilada nunca

Ciudad impenitente
Continúas

# City

Unloved city
Ravaged plaza
City forsaken

From revolt and plunder
From a plague of insects
From a fierce and ruthless rain
From unworthy residents
You rise up

City of exiles
City of penitents

Unloved city
City set alight
Never annihilated

Impenitent city
You carry on

# Crónicas

I

Entristecer es fácil. Basta un aire húmedo, un eco de lluvia o frío, una penumbra. Basta una campanada, lejos, dando la hora de la tarde, o un vestido azul o un párrafo. Como la muerte, la tristeza es un lugar común, una rutina. A quién le importa.

II

Dentro de mi cuerpo crece una rama envenenada. Una rama espinosa, lacerante, aguda ocupando lentamente mis venas, mi corazón, mis huesos.

Mi sangre es un veneno espeso, savia amarga y perfumada, ponzoña fluyendo lenta silenciosa.

Mi corazón se agrieta, se deforma, se hiende.

Debajo de los párpados una muerte ocupa lo mirado como un paisaje retorcido.

III

Figuras furtivas que pasan como un río oscuro.

Paraguas que se abren en mitad de la noche, bajo techo, sombras.

Sombras que atraviesan las paredes y convierten en sombra todo lo que tocan. Sombras que vagan sin prisas ni zozobras, tocando el miedo de los niños, ecos.

Ecos que no llegan a palabras, cáscaras vacías.

Pesadillas.

IV

Algo quiere arrancar esta tarde del mundo y arrancarnos. Caen filos, hojillas, largas agujas de hielo, uñas largas de rojo buscándole los ojos a la gente. Llueve un agua

# Chronicles

Grieving is easy. All it takes is a gust of humid air, an echo of rain or cold, the half-light. All it takes is a distant bell tolling its afternoon hours or a blue dress or a paragraph. Like death, sadness is commonplace, routine. What does it matter.

II

Within my body, a poisonous branch grows. A thorny, sharp, and lacerating branch that slowly fills my veins, my heart, my bones.

My blood is a thick venom, a bitter and fragrant sap, a flow of slow, silent poison.

My heart cracks, writhes, splits open.

Beneath my eyelids, a death fills the view like a gnarled landscape.

III

Furtive figures that pass like a black river.

Umbrellas that open indoors in the middle of the night, shadows.

Shadows that drift through the walls and turn all they touch to shadow. Shadows that roam without haste or angst, touching the children's fear, echoes.

Echoes that never become words, empty skins.

Nightmares.

IV

Something wants to rip this afternoon from the world, to rip us out. Blades, razors, and long needles of ice fall, long red claws searching for people's eyes.

voraz, desaforada, enloquecida. Los paraguas se agitan asustados como pequeños murciélagos expuestos a la luz. La lluvia es sempiterna y omnisciente. Demoledora, borra cualquier indicio, anula todo.

It rains a wild, hungry water. The umbrellas flap their wings like bats exposed to the light. The everlasting and omniscient rain, crushing, blots out any sign, revokes it all.

## Ninguna calle perdurará de ti

De tus calles, ninguna. Salgo de ti, ciudad mala anfitriona, mezquina y sola. Ni una puesta de sol, ni una sombra, ni un cielo, ni una flor.

De tus calles, ninguna. Salgo de ti ciudad sin ojos, ni siquiera ciega. Acaso ocultes muñones y jorobas, avergonzada, llagas y despojos. Acaso nada. No estás, no eres.

De tus calles, ninguna. Salgo de ti ciudad sin dones, ciudad que ni una piedra, ni un agua fresca, ni una forma de nube, ni un gato perdido.

De tus calles, ninguna. Salgo de ti ciudad incolora. Huyo de tus criaturas que cruzan las aceras con desgano, lanzando desperdicios y escupiendo y destilando tedio.

De tus calles, ninguna. Salgo de ti pobrecita ciudad sin esperanzas. Te dejo sin nostalgias, te dejo en el olvido.

De tus calles, ninguna. Salgo de ti ciudad sin danza ni relato. De ti ni un nombre, ni una plaza, ni una mañana, ni un café, ni un miedo. Ciudad sin moraleja ni posdata, nunca viví en ti, nadie ha vivido.

De tus calles, ninguna. Salgo de ti ciudad sin un latido, estéril. Aquí te dejo hasta el día en que te recojan los fantasmas, que los vientos te borren, que el agua se lleve tus casas. Aquí te dejo con tus fachadas sucias y tu sed. Agonizarás bajo el polvo, ciudad sin cantos, palabra muerta.

## No Street Will Survive You

Not one street will survive. I leave you, city, neglectful host, mean-spirited and alone. Not a sunset, not a shadow, not a sky, not even a flower.

Not one street will survive. I leave you, eyeless city, though you are not blind. You might shamefully hide amputations and kyphosis, ulcers and plunder. You might not. You don't exist, you are not.

Not one street will survive. I leave you, giftless city, city with neither a stone, a cloud formation, cool water, a missing cat.

Not one street will survive. I leave you, black-and-white city. I flee from your creatures that listlessly crisscross your sidewalks, littering and spitting and oozing boredom.

Not one street will survive. I leave you, impoverished and hopeless city. I leave you without nostalgia, I leave you in obscurity.

Not one street will survive. I leave you, city without stories or dances. From you, not even a name, not even a plaza, not even a morning, not even a café, not even fear. City with no moral at the end, not even a postscript, I never lived in you, nobody ever has.

Not one street will survive. I leave you, city without a heartbeat, barren. I leave you here until the day the ghosts come to collect you, until the winds erase you, until the water washes your houses away. I leave you here with your dirty facades and your thirst. Your death will rattle beneath the dust, songless city, dead word.

## Soledad

Trazo azul, línea larga, dibujo la mirada para enfrentar la calle
El rostro mío no, que no me vean.
Que el rostro de la soledad espanta
Azul bajo los ojos, agua
Este fondo que toco doloroso.

## Solitude

Blue stroke, long line, I draw a gaze to face the street
The face isn't my own, may they not see me
May this face of loneliness be frightening
Beneath the eyes, blue, water
This depth that I painfully touch.

## II

Contemplo lo que pasa y no me duelo
Nada me conmueve

Ni los vientres que albergan un monstruo pálido y hermoso
Ni el olor a veneno o a tumba en las paredes
Ni una flor abriendo suavemente su mentira blanquísima o rosada

Yo, rostro impasible
Contemplo lo que será derrumbe y arenero.

II


I watch what happens and do not grieve
Nothing moves me

Not the womb that harbors a pale and beautiful monster
Not the scent of poison or tomb in the wall
Not a flower smoothly opening its white or pink lies

I, unmoved face
I watch what will be landslide and sandpit.

# Naufragio

Naufragio
Embarcación pérdida
Arrojados a la orilla de nosotros mismos
Extenuados
Los que venimos del amor

Demasiado tristes para mirar el cielo, demasiado frágiles y tristes
Nosotros, los arrojados del amor
Sobrevivientes.

## Shipwreck

Shipwreck
Lost vessel
Cast to the shores of our selves
Exhausted
Those of us who come from love

Too sorrowful to see the sky, too frail and sorrowful
We, cast away by love
Survivors.

CIRO ROMERO

## [Dislocados reagrupamos los tumores]

Dislocados reagrupamos los tumores
se devuelve a la fisura
la sangre que quedó fuera del cuerpo
gotas, migas, abismo en torno a una cima
aparece la pregunta
sobre la manta la luz
colores reminiscencias
¿por dónde comenzamos a extrañar?
la náusea sucumbe se suspende
todas respuestas del antónimo
pelaje otoñal recambios lanudos
piel devorada melenas en el suelo
solo queda lo bélico
tejer o no las piedras
apartar el magma del pulmón
levitar sobre las aperturas del vientre
reconocer el parecido
la sangre que vuelve a recorrer las paredes de la grieta
el ruido de los huesos en el acantilado
rearmar.

## [Dislocated we regather the tumors]


Dislocated we regather the tumors
the blood that was spilled outside the body
is returned to the fissure
droplets, flakes of scab, the abyss around a mountaintop
a question appears
the light over the blanket
colors and memory
where is the place that we begin to miss?
nausea succumbs, suspends
everything is the antonym's answer
autumnal coat woolly replacements
devoured skin, mounds of fur across the ground
all that remains is warlike
weaving or not the stones
separating magma from lung
levitating above the womb's opening
recognizing the resemblance
the blood running up the walls of the crevice again
the clack of bones on the cliff top
reassembling.

## [El viaje es vertical]

El viaje es vertical
un paladar se parte como tiza

la sutura del hueso rebajada a hilos de sangre que el dedo traspasa
lonjas de piel abierta por la incursión

de a poco la figura demacrando la historia

      tensa el amarre
      desgarra la fibra

la gravedad emerge entre los orificios de la pelvis
y la inunda hasta que la tierra arropa

la garganta encoge su luz
un brazo se atasca en la úvula

mi índice atraviesa el paladar partido
se lastima apuntando la cumbre

se olvida y se empieza
una nueva mitad

tiempo como levadura hace crecer la asfixia
astillas entre los dientes amarran

raíces se enredan en lo hondo del esternón
ligamentos negados a supurar

eludir el asma

residuos pretenden reconstruir una ampolla
absorben temores de huesos

## [The journey is vertical]

The journey is vertical
the palate cracks like chalk

the suture of bone reduced to threads of blood and pierced by a finger
slices of skin opened by the attack

little by little the figure emaciates the story

   flexes against the lashings
   tears at the fiber

the weight rises between the pelvis's orifices
and it floods until the soil is soaked

the throat shrinks away its light
an arm is lodged in the uvula

my index finger punctures the split palette
and gets hurt pointing to the mountaintop

it is forgotten and it begins
a new half

time makes asphyxiation rise like leavening
splinters between the teeth tie down

roots that grow twisted deep in the sternum
ligaments unable to fester

avoiding asthma

the residues want to reconstruct a blister
and absorb the fear of the bones

otro intento antes de reposar la mano sobre la fosa
antes de dejar el brazo atrapado entre las vértebras

se olvida
se vuelve a empezar

hasta que la pulpa necrose.

another attempt before resting the hand above the pit
before leaving the arm trapped between vertebrae

forgotten
and beginning again

until the flesh rots.

## Exoesqueleto

I

La violencia de una noticia irrumpe
ojos digieren piel demacrada
la nueva distribución de los sonidos
      en base al vacío
      te golpea

¿excavarías en ti hasta conseguir el eje de la herida
levantarías la extremidad que debemos comenzar a olvidar
intercambiarías los pellejos por un bosque

por recorrer la forma
en que se voltean los días?

Cuál es el epicentro de las cosas
la costumbre de hacer de la gente sitios y huir
descifra el balbuceo de una lengua que se extingue
el discurso de un pulmón a punto de romperse

auscultan día por medio
qué invadió ayer la prisa
una oquedad espontánea se multiplica
      donde existían modos de esquivar

se resignan
tu instinto se degrada
curvamos la palabra evitando responder
escondemos la gravedad del tiempo
de una carne que hace su última danza

ahora estrenas pentágonos rugosos
una sonda se deslizó dentro de ti como parásito
lisa silente

# Exoskeleton

I

The violence of the news barges in
eyes digest gaunt skin
the new arrangement of sounds
      built on emptiness
      hits you

would you dig within yourself until you found the wound's axis?
would you lift the limb that we must begin to forget?
would you trade skin for a forest?

to walk the same direction
that the days turn?

What is the epicenter of these things?
the custom of making places of people and fleeing
deciphering the babbling of a dying tongue
the discourse of a lung on the point of collapse

they press their ears against the chest of every other day
what hurry invaded yesterday
a spontaneous and multiplying hole
      where avoidance once dwelled

they resign themselves
your instinct deteriorates
we arc the word to avoid responding
we hide the gravity of time
of a flesh that dances its last dance

now you debut rough pentagons
a probe slides into you like a parasite
smooth  soundless

la he visto entrar, salir
responder
estás a tiempo

el desastre es una noche hirviéndote en la frente

¿hay forma correcta de dejar caer?

si consigo el manantial
introduzco mi dedo
o alzo el temblor tan lejos
¿vendrías?
se deslizó al oído la imagen de tu mano aporreada

venas desembocan
el color del ruido se arrastra

deshaz los nudos
testigos sin nombres.

II

Te desprendes
niegas
no hay epicentro
desconoces
el cuerpo ahora es sordo
y el habla se incendia,
la arteria
una baranda
que la mirada alcance a cubrir
la escritura secundaria
herencia,
te vas
con tu tono y tus formas
te vas llamando
eso que no.

I've seen it go in and out
replying
you are on time

disaster is a night boiling on your forehead

is there a right way to fall?

if I find the wellspring
if I introduce my finger
or if I raise this trembling from so far away
would you come?
the image of your cudgeled hand slides into your ear

veins drain
the color of the noise crawls along

please   untie the knots
nameless witnesses.

II

you detach
and fill with denial
there is no epicenter
you disown
your body now deaf
and speech catches fire,
the artery
a railing
that your eyes reach for to cover
the secondary scripture
legacy,
you depart
with your tone and your form
you depart
calling that which doesn't call.

III

El duelo abandona cada extremo
un gesto punza, hurga
acaricia el reposo

la enfermedad te ocupó entre los cartílagos de las piernas y los discos de la espalda
después el follaje
invadió

pienso y no pienso en nada que no sea tu párpado pronunciando el cansancio
tu muerte es evidencia
el dolor nos apresa.

IV

Entre todos el retorno
tú desmembrada
dejada de tu decisión para buscar
reordenaremos tus capas según cada voluntad

¿el recuerdo o los alientos
en qué reencarnas?

La casa un apósito de dudas que daña, revienta los cálculos que no pronunciamos,
las columnas no sostienen el sonido de tus piernas, miembro horizontal de dos
colores. Barrí un último cabello entre las hojas, es temporal de lluvia y las grietas
de los muros el nuevo rostro.

Afuera, el recuerdo es el exoesqueleto que dejaste, la repetición las alas agitadas de
        [un insecto
la imagen y el sonido no viajan en la misma memoria
y nadie apura un cuerpo deshabitado

ahora la silueta conversa.

III

Pain abandons every extremity
a movement punctures through, digs around
caresses the stillness

the sickness filled you from the cartilage of your feet to the disks of your spine
afterward the foliage
invaded

I think and don't think of nothing may it not be your eyelid declaring its weariness
your death is evidence
pain seizes us.

IV

Together, the return
you, dismembered
abandoned by your choice to search
we'll reorganize the layers of your body according to every will

memory or breath?
into which will you be reincarnated?

The house, the dressed wound of damaging doubt, ruins our unsaid reckonings, the
columns can't support the sound of your legs, horizontal two-colored limb. I swept
up a final hair from among the leaves, it's now the era of rainstorms, of cracks in the
walls, the new face.

Outside, memory is the exoskeleton that you left behind, the litany of an insect's
        flapping wings
the image and the sound course through different memories
and nobody rushes an empty body

now the silhouette speaks.

## V

En el claustro
cultivada
describo
la forma de la oscuridad
inamovible
¿el frío está adentro o afuera?
las piedras prensan
el hueso respira
el resto del cuerpo perdió la inercia de opinar
volúmenes variables
escucho la palidez latiendo
la sangre pesa, es costra antes que río
los ojos se comenzaron a hundir
ahogados en el cráneo
delgada rigidez
las uñas caen por capas
una célula viva flota en el silencio
la boca apretada
y una larva explora las cuevas de los dientes
todo lo ordené alrededor de las orejas
única forma que recuerdo.
Temías.

V

In the cloister
I describe
the cultivated
immovable
shape of darkness
is the cold without or within?
the stones bear down
the bone breathes
the rest of your body has lost the inertia of speech
variable volumes
I listen to your throbbing pallor
the blood grows heavy, is scab before river
your eyes begin to sink
drowned in your skull
thin and rigid
fingernails flake off in layers
a living cell floats in the silence
your mouth pressed tight
and a larva explores the caverns of your teeth
I arranged everything around your ears
the only way I remember.
You were scared.

## [Tanto tiempo queriéndome ir que ya no sé cómo quedarme]

Tanto tiempo queriéndome ir que ya no sé cómo quedarme
recuerdo:

hombres, latidos, dedos que no son dedos,
somos
el estadio más larvario asentado sobre el fallo
irrevocable pálpito
la sensación final
el arrepentimiento de no habernos quedado para ver
hábitos inextirpables

recogería la tierra que desborda los senos
la mandíbula derramada sobre el tímpano
acurrucaría

me dejaré caer entre el tumulto hasta su cuenca vacía
y allí

quedarse.

# [So much time wanting to go that I no longer know how to stay]

So much time wanting to go that I no longer know how to stay
I remember:

men, heartbeats, fingers that aren't fingers
we are
larvae hanging above failure
irrevocable feeling
the final sensation
the regret of not having stuck around to see
unstoppable habits

I'd gather up the soil that brims from the breasts
the jawbone that spills over the eardrum
I'd curl up beside them

I'll let myself fall through the turmoil to that empty basin
and there

I'll stay.

GEORGINA RAMÍREZ

## Extranjera

Soy inmigrante en mi cuerpo

¿dónde el rostro
una mueca quizá,
algún trazo?

Intento extraer los restos

ni siquiera una mano
para asirme al recuerdo
ni un diente para morder la herida

mi silueta
apenas una sombra

un breve instante si te nombro

## Foreigner

I'm an immigrant in my body

Where's my face,
somewhere, an expression?
Any trace? Any sign?

I try to save what remains

but not even a hand
to hold on to memory
nor teeth to bite the wound

my silhouette
hardly a shadow

a brief moment if I name you

## Daño oculto

Me dejo caer en gotas sobre su lengua

Se entrega a pedazos
le devuelvo el gesto

A veces intuye que no soy suya
y me enternece

Los domingos
viene cargando abedules para mi vientre
y un trébol azul que me corre hasta los pies

Me bebo su calma cuando se duerme
le dejo toda la nostalgia en la espalda
me abrazo a sus sueños

entiendo
que aún no es el momento de decirle
que ya me he ido

## Hidden Damage

I fall in drops over your tongue

you surrender until only pieces are left
I do the same

Sometimes you sense that I'm not yours
and it softens me

On Sundays
You come bearing birch trees for my womb
and a blue clover that runs down to my feet

I drink your calm as you sleep
Upon my back I leave you all my longing
I embrace your dreams

I understand
that even though it's not time to tell you
I've already gone

## La parada del colibrí

Tengo urgencia de tus labios
salgo a buscarte
en cualquier tormenta

Me bebo los cuerpos
que atraviesan esta nostalgia
las horas se hacen infinitas
en ese reloj no compartido

Me pierdo
en encuentros divergentes
hago de mi entrega
el más infeliz de todos los boleros

## The Hummingbird's Stop

I thirst for your lips
I go searching for you
in any storm

I drink the bodies
that pierce this desire
the hours become infinite
in that unshared clock

I lose myself
in fleeting encounters
From my devotion I sing
the unhappiest of all boleros

# Ráfaga

Anclo en la vieja herida
la ato a un costado
sus labios cubro con bocas nuevas

desaparece

Pero alguien dice *recuerda*

hago el recorrido vertical por la memoria
y la gota se hace eco
bordeando tu nombre

Sangra

el invierno regresa

## Gust

I drop anchor in the old wound
I tie it to one side
I cover its lips with new mouths

it vanishes

But somebody says *remember*

I take the memory's vertical voyage
and the droplet echoes
along the shores of your name

It bleeds

The winter returns

## Noviembre cuarto

Hoy ha muerto mi padre

solo el movimiento de mis labios
recuerda tierra

me hago nube

en casa pequeñas islas
naufragamos en intemperie

su aliento menguó
entre mis brazos
fragmentando el suelo

cerrando mis ojos con él

## November Fourth

My father died today

only the movement of my lips
remembers the ground

I become a cloud

small islands at home
we're shipwrecked in the elements

his breath slows
between my arms
fragmenting the land

closing my eyes with him

## Intemperie

Él le regala su último adiós
La despide con la mirada envejecida
como quien ha visto tanto amanecer a su lado
que conoce todas las noches de su cuerpo

Ella le sujeta el alma
la anuda con palabras que ya no dicen
que son solo errancia
Promete otra noche
una última noche estragada que no sepa de mañanas
que estalle en el temblor de las carnes

Hay recuerdos que no saben despedirse

## Elements

He says his final farewell
sends her off with an aged glance
like someone who's seen so many dawns at his side
who knows all the nights of his body

She grips his spirit
knots it with words no longer said
they are only wandering
She promises another night
a final ravaged night that knows nothing of morning
which shatters in the trembling of flesh

These memories that don't know how to say goodbye

## Plegaria

Dónde los deditos de tus manos
niño triste
tarareando una canción
racimos púrpura
los gestos de tus brazos

La noche
engulle la miseria que desgarra tu día

Tañes tu sonrisa
a la tierra
que te arrulla
amamanta tu insomnio

Duerme niño
en tu cama de cemento
refúgiate del frío
que sirvan para algo
los periódicos de mi país

## Prayer

Where are your little fingers
sad child
humming yourself a song
those purple clusters
the movement of your arms

The night
swallows the misery that mangles your day

Your smile strums
to the earth
who coos you to sleep
nursing your insomnia

Sleep child
in your concrete bed
may you find shelter from the cold
may the newspapers of my country
be good for something

## Reo número 329727

Reposa el hombre a la espera
marioneta de su destino

solo un suelo pestilente cobija el sueño

Piensa en la madre
su sexo en venta para el sustento
y ese afán de protegerlo de las calles
obligado resguardo del desamparo

Mil cruces no bastaron para bendecirlo

Entrar descalzo al calabozo—ordenan—
en este inframundo
un par de trenzas pueden zanjar la vida

Qué entienden los zapatos de libertad

## Prisoner No. 329727

The man leans back and waits
a marionette to his destiny

Only a filthy floor covers his dream

He thinks of his mother
selling sex for sustenance
trying to save him from the streets
a forced shelter from neglect

A thousand crosses couldn't bless him

He enters the cell barefoot—as they order—
in this underworld
a pair of shoelaces can settle this question of life

What do shoes know of liberty?

## En el semáforo

Ellos te miran
esconden sus miedos
lavados al sol

la armadura de cristal
separa su hambre
de tu duda

Inevitable la luz verde

## At the Traffic Light

They look your way
hiding their fear
awash in sunlight

a glass shield
divides their hunger
from your doubt

The green light imminent

## Credo

No basta una plegaria
divagar en la tiniebla te ha extraviado
he nadado en la locura
y en tu nombre
madre
hoy me confieso
De pronto tus alas desconocieron el vuelo
y estalla en la ventana el mañana
la luz se hace miedo
te pierdo
No supe de esta oscuridad que eras
y deshago los peldaños que me llevan a tu infierno
ya no hay camino en ti
Se diluyen los días que te nombran
Nunca has sabido levar anclas
quizá por eso el naufragio
la deriva en los ojos

## Creed

A prayer isn't enough
you lost your way wandering through the shadows
I've swum in madness
and in your name
Mother
today I confess
Suddenly your wings disowned flight
and tomorrow shatters in the window
the light turns into fear
I lose you
I knew nothing of the darkness you once were
and I level the stairs that brought me to your hell
In you there is still no path
The days that name you dissolve
You never knew how to lift anchor
and so the shipwreck
the drift in your eyes

## 4900 kilómetros

Perdona que te llene la tierra de nostalgia
estoy anegada y me desbordo
Mi país hoy es un animal herido
y yo muerdo por él
Somos llaga
lamento
y exilio
llevamos un dolor en los hombros
Queremos ser sonrisa
lo juro
pero la boca se niega a esbozar el gesto
porque en mi país hay hambre
y yo no puedo dormir
con tanto estómago vacío
Mis niños mueren
en las calles y en los hospitales
porque alguien decidió que esas vidas no valen
y los encarcelan
aunque no lo creas
a mis niños los ponen tras las rejas
y les pegan
y ellos no entienden
así no se juega a los soldaditos
mis niños sufren
y por eso hoy
yo que estoy lejos
inundo tu tierra
con mi llanto

## 4,900 Kilometers

*Caracas to Santiago as the crow flies*

Sorry that the land fills you with longing
I'm flooded and I overflow
Today my country is a wounded animal
and I bite on its behalf
We are sores
lamentation
and exile
We carry pain across our shoulders
We want to be smile
I swear
but our mouth refuses
because in my country there's hunger
and I can't sleep
with so many empty stomachs
My children are dying
in the streets and in the hospitals
because somebody declared their lives worthless
and they imprison them
though you may not believe it
they lock my children behind bars
and they beat them
and they don't understand
this isn't how one plays with toy soldiers
My children suffer
and for that today
I who am so far away
drown your land
with my tears

## Un poema llamado país

No es solo partir
y dejar el hambre en las esquinas
Es escuchar en tu idioma
palabras ajenas
Explicar la miseria que te curte la piel
y te inunda la mirada
Defender la dignidad
de las siete estrellas tatuadas
Sí
partir es partirse
van pedazos de ti
sin ti
recorriendo caminos
que no conducen
Partes con el hambre de todos
en la espalda
y cada bocado duele
por el que nada
lleva a la boca
y buscas algún sabor
que llene tanto vacío
Así se parte
así nos partimos
mientras vamos en trenes
que nunca llegarán a casa

## A Poem Called Country

It's more than just leaving
and saying goodbye to hunger on the street corners
It's hearing strange words
in your own language
It's explaining the misery that tans your skin
and floods your gaze
It's defending the dignity
of your seven-starred tattoo
It's true
Leaving means letting pieces
of yourself go
on without you
They wander on foot
through streets they cannot drive
You leave carrying everyone's
hunger on your back
and every bite aches
through the nothingness
that you bring to your mouth
You search for any flavor
that might fill so much emptiness
This is how we go
This is how we're broken
as we leave in trains
that will never arrive home

# CONTRIBUTORS

**Ivana Aponte** (b. Caracas, Venezuela, 1990) earned a degree in literature from the Universidad Católica Andrés Bello in Caracas and a master's degree in literature from the University of Chile. She is a copyeditor, independent editor, and teacher of Spanish as a foreign language. Her poems have been published in *Orquídeas voces: Muestra de poesía venezolana contemporánea, Letralia, La Parada Poética, Pruka, Los Poetas del 5,* and the anthologies *Me Vibra II: Brevísima antología arbitraria Panamá: Venezuela* (2020) and *Una cicatriz donde se escriben despedidas: Antología de poesía venezolana en Chile* (2021). Her collection *Afectos* was published by LP5 Editora in 2022. She has lived in Santiago, Chile, since 2017.

**Lorena Caraballo** (b. Caracas, Venezuela, 1989) earned a technical degree in graphic design from the Instituto Universitario de Diseño Las Mercedes (IUDLM) in 2013. She is a writer and editor of nonfiction articles, narrative fiction, and poetry. She has written film-related articles for the Venezuelan National Cinematheque as well as fashion and lifestyle articles for *Velvet Magazine Latinoamérica.* Her work has also appeared in blogs and on literary websites such as *Sympathy for the Libro* and *Digo.palabra.txt.* Since 2018, she has lived in Santiago, Chile, where she works as a Spanish-English interpreter.

**Fergie Contreras Salmen** (b. Isla de Margarita, Venezuela, 1993) earned a law degree from the Universidad de los Andes in Venezuela and a master's degree in editing from the Universidad Diego Portales in Chile. Her first poetry collection, *Mundo a escala,* was published in Chile in 2021.

**Elizaria Flores** (b. Caracas, Venezuela, 1961) was formerly a professor in the Department of Humanities at the Universidad de los Andes in Venezuela. She is a poet, linguist, and textile artist who holds a degree in Hispanoamerican and Venezuelan literature. Her poems have been published in *Letralia, Cuadrivium,*

*Actual-Universidad de Los Andes,* and *El Salmón.* Her poetry collection received an honorable mention for the biennial DAES award from the Universidad de los Andes. She is the author of *El torpe andar,* published by LP5 Editora in 2022.

**Miguel A. Hernández Zambrano** (b. Maracaibo, Venezuela, 1983) holds a bachelor's degree in Spanish from the University of Zulia and an MFA in creative writing in Spanish from New York University. His books include *Antología del descapotable* (2006); *Cotidiano* (2010); *Un decir errado,* which won an honorable mention in the Concurso Nacional de Poesía Delia Rengifo (2012); and *¡Oh, lorem ipsum!* (2014), awarded the IV National Poetry Contest prize in Venezuela. He lives in Santiago, Chile.

**Gladys Mendía** (b. Maracay, Venezuela, 1975) holds degrees in tourism and literature. Highlights of her work as a Portuguese-to-Spanish translator include *La catedral del desorden* (ARC Edições, 2017), an anthology of poetry by Roberto Riva. She was the recipient of a fellowship from La Fundación Pablo Neruda in Valparaíso, Chile, in 2003. Her books include *El tiempo es la herida que gotea* (2009); *El alcohol de los estados intermedios* (2009); *La silenciosa desesperación del sueño* (2010); *La grita* and *El barco ebrio* (2011); *Las inquietantes dislocaciones del pulso* (2012); and *Trizadura ediciones* (2018). Her most recent book, *El cantar de los manglares* (2018), was published in English as *The Singing of the Mangroves* (2019). Her work has been translated into Catalan, Portuguese, English, French, and Swedish. She is the founding editor of *Los Poetas del 5* and the cofounder of La Furia del Libro. As an editor, she has published twelve anthologies that highlight binational and bicontinental poets.

**Miguel Ortiz Rodríguez** (b. Caracas, Venezuela, 1993) holds a degree from the Escuela de letras in la Universidad Católica Andrés Bello. His poems have been published in *Stand Up Poetry* (Venezuela), *Cantera* (Venezuela), *Ojo* (Venezuela), *Canibalismos* (Venezuela), *Sinécdoque* (Venezuela), *Caligrama* (Spain), *Furman* (United States), and *Digo.palabra.txt* (Venezuela). His work also appeared in the anthology *102 poetas jamming* (2014). He was a finalist in the I Certamen Mundial Excelencia Literaria in the United States and in the I Concurso de Prosa Poética Ojos Verdes Ediciones in Alicante, Spain.

**Georgina Ramírez** (b. Caracas, Venezuela, 1972) has a degree in social work and specializes in group dynamics and art therapy. She is the creator and director of

*La Parada Poética.* Her poems have been published in anthologies such as *El ojo errante* (Venezuela); *La mujer rota* (Mexico); *La voz de la ciudad* (Venezuela); *Miradas y palabras sobre Caracas, para bien o para mal* (Venezuela); *Arte poética* (Argentina); *Cien mujeres contra la violencia de género* (Venezuela); *102 poetas jamming* (Venezuela); *El puente es la palabra* (Venezuela); *Aquel invierno que gritamos* (Spain); *La mujer rota* (Dominican Republic), and *Fragua de preces* (Spain). Her published collections include *Piel de durazno* (2010), *Lo que calla la noche* (2015), and *Daño oculto* (2015). She lives in Santiago, Chile.

**Gerardo Arístides Rivodó** (b. Caracas, Venezuela, 1978) studied literature at the Universidad Central de Venezuela. Their poetry was published in *Tal Cual* in 2013. They won the Por una Venezuela Literaria contest in 2017. In 2018, Le Chien Editor in New York published their poetry collection, *Pájaros de Haldol.* They live in Santiago, Chile.

**Ciro Romero** (b. Valencia, Venezuela, 1993) graduated with a degree in dentistry in 2016. He was a finalist in the Concurso Nacional de Poesía Joven Rafael Cadenas. He lives in Santiago, Chile.

**Maximiliano Sojo** (b. Caracas, Venezuela, 1990) studied English and French pedagogy at the Universidad Pedagógica Experimental Libertador and works as an English teacher in Santiago, Chile. He has been published in *Digo.palabra.txt* and in the special edition of *Awen* (2018). In 2018, his work received an honorable mention in the III Concurso Nacional de Poesía Rafael Cadenas. His poetry has appeared in *Alba Londres* and has been anthologized in the *Antología del II Festival Internacional de Poesía de Santiago* (2019). He is the cofounder of Fundación Versolibre, a nonprofit organization that promotes the reading and writing of poetry in Chile.

**Eva Tizzani** (b. Coro, Venezuela, 1995) has published her poetry in *Jóvenes Creadores, Poémame, L'Accordéon, Espejismos del Trópico, Ácracia pour les porcs, Poesía desde Valencia, Iberoamérica, Letralia, Los Poetas del 5,* and *Grifo.* Her poem "[Dead moths]" won third place in the Certamen de Poesía Venezolana Ecos de la Luz contest.

**Julio Tizzani** (b. Coro, Venezuela, 1990) lives in southern Chile, where he works as a surgeon. His poems have been published in *Letralia* and *Grifo.* His collection *Árbol genealógico* appeared in 2018.

**Fernando Vanegas** (b. San Cristóbal, Venezuela, 1992) holds a degree in Spanish and literature from the Universidad de los Andes. He won the Primer Concurso Estadal Juvenil de Cuentos of Táchira in 2010 and the Premio DAES Concurso Literario de Cuento, Ensayo y Poesía from the Universidad de los Andes, Mérida, in 2011. He is a member and cofounder of the literary collective Los Hijos del Lápiz. He was the winner of the fiction writers' contest of the Fondo Editorial Simón Rodríguez magazine in Táchira in 2012. His poem "Un hogar entre las piedras" was published in *Los Poetas del 5* (2018).

**Sara Emanuel Viloria** (b. Maracaibo, Venezuela, 1990) earned a fine arts degree from the Universidad Centroccidental Lisandro Alvarado. She works as a professional artist and designer in Santiago, Chile, alternating between visual art and editorial projects. Her poetry has been published in the United States and Spain and has been anthologized in the *Antología del II Festival Internacional de Poesía de Santiago* (2019) and published in two chapbooks by *Los Poetas del 5* (2018). She has designed books such as *Poeta en Nueva York* (García Lorca), *Antología de la novísima poesía larense* (Venezuelan poetry), and *Antología del II Festival Internacional de Poesía de Santiago* (2019).